Speak Up
and Get Along!

Learn The Mighty Might, Thought Chop,
and More Tools To Make Friends,
Stop Teasing, and Feel GOOD About Yourself

BY SCOTT COOPER

ILLUSTRATED BY JOE FOURNIER

free spirit
PUBLISHING®

Library of Congress Cataloging-in-Publication Data
Cooper, Scott.
    Speak up and get along! : learn the mighty might, thought chop, and more tools to make friends, stop teasing, and feel good about yourself / Scott Cooper.
       p. cm.
    Includes bibliographical references and index.
    ISBN 1-57542-182-8
1. Interpersonal communication—Juvenile literature. 2. School children—Conduct of life—Juvenile literature. I. Title.
    BF637.C45C687 2005
    158.2'083'4—dc22   2005004431

ISBN: 978-1-57542-182-7

Thanks to the National Crime Prevention Council for use of the McGruff the Crime Dog® art on page 70.

The swimming metaphor referred to on pages 104–110 is from *Best Friends, Worst Enemies: Understanding the Social Lives of Children* by Michael Thompson, Ph.D., and Catherine O'Neill Grace with Lawrence J. Cohen, Ph.D., copyright © 2001 by Michael Thompson, Ph.D., and Catherine O'Neill Grace. Used by permission of Ballantine Books, an imprint of Random House, a division of Penguin Random House LLC. All rights reserved.

Reading Level Grade 4; Interest Level Ages 8–12;
Fountas & Pinnell Guided Reading Level S

Edited by Eric Braun
Cover design by Marieka Heinlen
Interior design by Percolator
Illustrated by Joe Fournier

20 19 18 17 16
Printed in the United States of America
V20300917

Free Spirit Publishing Inc.
6325 Sandburg Road, Suite 100
Minneapolis, MN 55427-3674
(612) 338-2068
help4kids@freespirit.com
www.freespirit.com

FSC
www.fsc.org
MIX
Paper from responsible sources
FSC® C005010

Free Spirit offers competitive pricing.
Contact edsales@freespirit.com for pricing information on multiple quantity purchases.

DEDICATION
To Adam, Jackson, and Brooke

ACKNOWLEDGMENTS

Sincere thanks to those who shared their ideas and expertise, listed here alphabetically:

Cordelia Anderson, M.A., speaker, trainer, and consultant to schools on promoting well-being and preventing harmful behaviors, including bullying and violence prevention; Stefanie Capps, superintendent of the Dunham School District in northern California; Thomas S. Greenspon, Ph.D., licensed psychologist and licensed marriage and family therapist; Sam Humleker, seventh grader at Ramsey International Fine Arts Center, Minneapolis, Minnesota; Scott Mahoney, Ed.D., superintendent of the Waugh School District in northern California; Dorothea M. Ross, Ph.D., past research psychologist in the Division of Behavioral and Developmental Pediatrics at the University of California, San Francisco; KaTrina Wentzel, M.Ed., fifth and ninth grade teacher in St. Paul, Minnesota, and past curriculum coordinator and diversity director; all the kids who reviewed and commented on the material; and my wife, Julie, for her very helpful review and input.

Thanks also to the great people at Free Spirit Publishing and their commitment to helping children: my very talented editor Eric Braun, editorial director Marjorie Lisovskis, Douglas Fehlen, and special thanks to Judy Galbraith for providing the opportunity to publish this book.

CONTENTS

Introduction

School can be a lot of fun. It's great to learn new things and hang out with friends. But school can also be hard—and not just because you have to learn fractions, world history, or how to play C-sharp on the trumpet. It's hard because you've got to work, play, and spend all your time with other kids and adults. You have to get along with people:

- in class
- in the hallways
- on the playground
- in the gym
- on the bus
- and just about everywhere else.

That's a lot of getting along! And sometimes it's tough, because all those people have their own thoughts, feelings, and needs.

One way to make getting along easier is to show respect for others. Respecting other people means thinking of them as important individuals, accepting them, and treating them the way you'd like to be treated. Showing respect for yourself is just as important as having it for others. Always remember that YOU are an important person. If you treat others and yourself with respect, people will usually treat you with respect, too. This book can help make that happen:

It will teach you to **speak up** for yourself and others in a respectful way...

...so you can **get along**—with others AND yourself.

WHAT DO BIRDS HAVE TO DO WITH GETTING ALONG?

Part of respecting others is not judging them before you know them. When I was younger, I had a prejudged idea about people who watched birds. I thought of them as, well . . . nerdy. I pictured bird watchers as people who wore high socks, funny-looking hats, and binoculars dangling from their necks.

I kept that image even after I became an adult, and my brothers had started bird watching. Then one day my brothers invited me to join them, and I discovered that I liked it. Bird watching (or *birding,* as many people prefer to call it) was a new and exciting world to me. I found out that I enjoyed being with other birders, and that they were nice, regular people (even if some of them did wear goofy hats). That experience showed me that even adults can learn more about respecting each other and getting along.

Since then I've learned more about birds. I've learned that most are very good at communicating, or telling each other things. Because they often live in flocks or small groups, they need to communicate in order to get along. They don't use words, but they use calls and songs that tell each other what they need and don't like. Baby birds peep for food and help. Adult birds give out sharp warning calls if danger is near and sing beautiful songs to attract mates. Young birds learn the songs and sounds they will need from the adult birds that raise them.

All those songs and sounds are tools birds need to help them get along and take care of themselves. And you know what? Kids also need communication tools to help them get along with others and take care of themselves. That's why I wrote *Speak Up and Get Along!*

HOW TO USE THIS BOOK

Each chapter in this book teaches you a different set of tools to help you with a different part of speaking up and getting along. And each chapter is named after a kind of different bird that is good at that set of tools. You can choose the chapters and tools to help you with situations or problems you're dealing with. For example, if you're being teased at school, you can go to the chapter called "Stopping Teasing and Bullying: The Tools of the Hummingbird." Hummingbirds are really good at standing up for themselves, even against bigger animals. Or, if you're feeling bad about yourself and having trouble getting things done, you can read the chapter called "Talking Back to Negative Thoughts: The Tools of the Owl." Owls can see clearly, even when things seem dark.

You'll get the most use out of this book if you read it from beginning to end and practice all the tools. Practice by yourself, with friends, and with adults you trust, who can share some of their own ideas and experiences. Boxes that say "Practice Time" will teach you a specific way to practice a tool.

People are *social*. That means we spend most our time with other people. *Speak Up and Get Along!* focuses mainly on school, because school is the place where you're most often on your own in social situations. But the tools you'll learn here don't just work at school. They work wherever you're with other people, including at home, in your neighborhood, and out and about. It's important to get along no matter where you are.

As a kid, I didn't like it when I saw people bullied, so I would try to help them. As an adult, it's even harder for me to see kids being mistreated. But there is a lot you can do on your own to make difficult situations better. You have great strength. You also have teachers, principals, parents, and other caring adults who want to help you if things get really tough.

Most of the time, getting along is easy and fun. It's fun to talk, hang out, play games, study, and be on teams with people. It's fun to help others and work together. For those times when getting along is not so easy, *Speak Up and Get Along!* can help you.

I'd like to know how these tools work for you. Write to me and let me know if they helped you speak up and get along, and tell me about other tools you have found.

Scott Cooper

You can email me at:
help4kids@freespirit.com

Or you can send me a letter in care of:
Free Spirit Publishing
6325 Sandburg Road, Suite 100
Minneapolis, MN 55427-3674

Expressing Yourself

THE TOOLS OF THE BLUE JAY

Blue jays are squawking, jabbering birds. If you walk into any forest in North America, you're bound to hear a blue jay or one of its jay cousins. If a blue jay doesn't like what other birds are doing, it's very loud in telling them so. If it needs help from another blue jay, it asks for it by quickly calling out. Blue jays set a good example for how to tell others what you want and how you feel, and to ask for help when you need it.

All living creatures have ways to communicate. Mother birds chirp to warn their babies, dogs yelp when they're in pain, cats purr when they're content, and guinea pigs stand on their heads and plug their ears when they're angry (just kidding). But no other living creature is able to communicate as completely as humans, because humans have words. We can use our words to talk, holler, sing, or cheer, and we can write our words on paper or a computer.

Words are a great way to communicate because words are so specific. If a dog whines, we don't know if it's hungry, sad, or just wants to go outside. But with words, people can tell others exactly what they mean. For example, "I'll take a double cheeseburger with Swiss cheese, pickles, tomatoes, lettuce—and *no onion!*"

WHEN TO USE THE TOOLS OF THE BLUE JAY

Telling other people exactly what you mean is especially important when you're not getting along with those people. For example, if someone takes your favorite eraser, you can use words to tell that person to give it back. And if someone says something mean to you, you can say right back that you don't like it. And you can say why, too.

Difficulties getting along with people are sometimes called *social problems.* Social problems often happen when people don't show enough respect for each other. Check out how two students reacted when they didn't get enough respect.

RASHEED was shooting baskets when Michael ran up and grabbed his basketball. "Come and get it, slowpoke," he taunted.

Rasheed felt furious. Basketball tryouts were tomorrow, and he really needed to practice. Besides, Michael was *always* doing things like this. It made Rasheed want to explode. "Give me that ball back, now!" he yelled. But Michael just

CONTINUED ⟶

laughed. Rasheed had had enough. He charged at Michael and tackled him. As the ball rolled off the court, the two boys wrestled on the hard blacktop.

Later, they slouched in chairs in the principal's office. Michael had a dark, swollen eye, Rasheed had a bloody nose, and they both had scraped knuckles and bruises all over. Both were suspended from school. Worse, Rasheed would not be allowed to try out for the basketball team. "But I didn't start this," Rasheed pleaded.

"That doesn't matter," the principal responded.

BRENDA loved her art class. She especially enjoyed painting watercolors and making pottery. But there was one thing she didn't like. Every day she was the only one to clean the mess at her group's table. There were drippy paint brushes, sopping paper towels, and broken pieces of clay. She worried that if she spoke up, the other kids in the group might not like her. But if the table wasn't cleaned, their group would lose points for their semester grades. Brenda wanted the other kids at the table to like her, and she didn't want to lose points, so she always cleaned up. She knew it wasn't fair, though, and it was starting to make art less fun.

Rasheed and Brenda didn't get the respect they deserved, and they ended up doing things they regretted. When you have trouble getting along with others, you may feel like fighting, like Rasheed did, or avoiding the problem, like Brenda did. Those reactions are natural. But neither reaction will help you in the long run. If you fight, you can hurt yourself or others, and you can get in trouble. Fighting can ruin friendships and make problems worse. If you ignore a problem, it usually won't go away. The people you're not getting along with may get their way—even if they're being unfair or unkind. And the next time you see them, the problem is right back again. You've taught them that they don't have to give you respect.

Rasheed and Brenda would have been better off if they had expressed themselves about what they didn't like. To express yourself, you need to be assertive. Being assertive doesn't mean being tough or mean, and it doesn't mean starting a fight. So what does it mean?

Being **assertive** means sticking up for yourself and others. It means **asking** for what you need or deserve in a strong, confident way.

Sometimes kids may be mean to you, they may try to get you to do things you don't really want to do, or they may try to keep you from getting things that you deserve. Most of the time, the best thing to do if you are not getting along with another person is to *talk* to that person. You will probably have to be assertive to get the respect you deserve. The tools of the Blue Jay can help you.

TooL #1

The Power I

*Use the Power I to tell others what you think, what you want,
or how you feel when they are not treating you fairly.*

The Power I is a simple but powerful tool: it means using an "I" sentence that is strong and direct. If someone does something mean, you can say, "I want you to stop doing that," or, "I don't like that." If you disagree with someone, this is also a good time to use the Power I. Tell that person, "I don't agree with that," or, "I have a different opinion."

WAYS TO SAY IT: THE POWER I

The person who sits behind you at school keeps thumping your head with a pencil.
Power I: *Hey, I want you to cut it out!*

You've been waiting to swing on the swings for a long time, but another person won't stop swinging.
Power I: *I want to use the swings, too. I've been waiting a long time, so please let me on now.*

The Power I can be even simpler. You don't even have to say the "I" out loud. You can keep it inside of you. If someone is calling you names, you can simply say, "Please stop it." What you are really saying is, "I want you to please stop it." But to keep it simple you can keep the "I" inside.

MORE WAYS TO SAY IT: THE POWER I

A kid cuts in front of you in line.
Power I: *Be fair. The line starts back there.*

Your teacher has assigned a group of you to write a report, but you are the only one doing any work.

Power I: *The assignment is that we write this as a group. Let's figure out how each of us can help.*

A kid teases you for having a pimple.

Power I: *Leave me alone!*

----------- Body Talk -----------

Not all your communication happens through words. Your face and body communicate, too. This is called *body language.* When you have a big smile, others know you're happy. When you have a scowl on your face, people know you're angry.

Sometimes your words say one thing and your body says another. For example, if you say, "I'm very happy," but your mouth is frowning, people will usually believe your frown more than your words. Or if you say, "I'm not afraid," but your knees are shaking and your eyes are bulging, your body language is telling a different story.

When you're using the Power I, it's important to use body language that shows that you mean what you say. If you act afraid, other people may not take you seriously. If you act mean or tough, they may think you are starting a fight. Instead:

- Stand tall.
- Hold your head high.
- Pull your shoulders back.
- Look the person in the eye.
- Don't move away.

Your tone of voice is also important. Speak calmly in a strong, clear voice. Don't yell, but don't talk too quietly, either. With the right body language and tone of voice, you show that you are firm and serious.

TOO MEAN   TOO SCARED   ASSERTIVE

USING THE POWER I WITH AUTHORITY FIGURES

It can be hard to use the Power I with older kids or adults. You might worry that they will get angry or make fun of you. You might think that they won't listen to you. You might even be afraid that they will hurt you.

When it comes time to use the Power I with authority figures like teachers and parents, it's natural to be nervous. But remember that no matter who you are talking to, you have the right to be respected. Sometimes adults have to hear what your needs are. There are two things you can do to make it easier to speak up in these situations. One is to say how hard it is to speak openly and honestly. Another is to express how you think they might feel about what you have to say. Here are some examples to help you get started:

I hate to make a big deal, but I need to tell you that . . .

I'm worried you might feel bad hearing this, but I want . . .

It's hard for me say this, but I don't think that . . .

You may not like this, but I want you to . . .

Maybe nobody else has told you this, but I . . .

Remember, it's important to be respectful toward adults and other authority figures, even when you're being assertive.

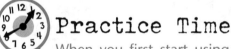 Practice Time

When you first start using the Power I, you might feel nervous with kids your own age, too. This is also normal. It can be hard to tell people things you know they might not want to hear. If you're nervous, practice the Power I with a good friend or an adult you trust. With your practice partner, make up some situations in which people act disrespectful toward you. (Or think of a real problem in your life, a situation where you'd like to be more assertive.) Then come up with several ways of using the Power I to speak up for your right to respect. Take turns saying the lines to each other. With practice, the Power I will become easier and easier, and telling others how you feel will begin to feel natural. ■

Here's one last point about the Power I: be polite. This is very important. You're asking people to treat you with respect, and they deserve to be treated that way, too. You may be angry, but being mean won't help you. The Power I works best when you use it in a polite but firm way.

TooL #2

The No Thanks

Use the No Thanks to say no to people who pressure you.

Have friends ever tried to get you to do things you didn't want to do? Has anyone tried to talk you into something you knew was unsafe or wrong? For example, maybe someone tried to pressure you into being mean to somebody else. Or maybe someone tried to talk you into taking something that wasn't yours. A big part of having respect for yourself is keeping yourself safe and out of trouble. And that means learning to say no to bad situations.

ASTRID was starting to be accepted by the most popular group of girls in her class. She sat with them at pep rallies and at lunch. For the first time, she'd been invited to a boy-girl party.

At the party, Astrid and her friends stood talking near the stereo. Linda looked around to see if any adults were nearby, then pulled a small bottle of liquor from her bag. "Try a little," she said, "it'll make you feel dizzy." Astrid was surprised but also curious. The girls giggled and took sips. Other kids were watching. Astrid's mom had talked to her about not drinking alcohol. She knew she should say no, but Astrid didn't want to fall out of the popular group. She was confused and nervous.

Someone passed her the bottle. Astrid took a deep breath and said, "No thanks. I'm good."

Sometimes, because you want others to like you, you might be tempted to say yes to things you really don't want to do. You might even say yes to things that you know you shouldn't do. You probably know that it's very important to say no to things like:

- drugs
- tobacco
- violence
- stealing
- cheating
- being mean to others
- movies and Internet sites that aren't meant for kids

You probably also know it's not always easy to say no.

Kids who are your own age are called your *peers*. When peers try to get you to do things that they're doing, that's called *peer pressure,* and it can be very hard to resist. People naturally want to be liked, and doing things that friends ask seems like an easy way to get them to like you.

Even good friends might try to talk you into things you're not sure about. Maybe they just want you to go to parties, movies, or other activities that you're not interested in. Or they may try to get you to do something dangerous.

But you'll be happier and safer—and you'll show self-respect—if you think and act independently. You can make your own choices and say no to other kids when you need to. That's where another simple tool comes in: the No Thanks. The No Thanks just means saying no when you need to.

Like using the Power I, saying no to friends, older kids, and adults can make you nervous or uncomfortable. You might worry about hurting another person's feelings, or about being teased or not being liked. You might be afraid of making the other person angry or disappointed.

For worries like these, here are three things that can make saying no easier:

1. **Self-respect.** This is the biggest help. If you have respect for yourself, you know you're too important to risk your safety. You also know you are the best person to make decisions about yourself.

2. **Honesty.** Be honest about how nervous you are, even as you're saying no. For example, you can say something like, "I don't want you to feel bad, but I've just got to say no," or, "I like being with you, but I can't do this."

3. **A "No" Buddy.** Get a friend to back you up. If your "No" Buddy says no right along with you, it can be a lot easier—for both of you.

 Practice Time

If you have been pressured to do something you don't feel good about doing, you can make a plan with your "No" Buddy for the next time it happens. Before you see the kids who are pressuring you, make an agreement with your friend that you will both say no. Come up with ways of using the No Thanks and practice them on each other. Then, when the time comes and you're feeling pressured, back each other up! ■

WAYS TO SAY IT: THE NO THANKS

If you're worried about hurting feelings

No. I wish I could, but I can't.

That's really nice, but I have to say no.

No, but thanks for asking.

I'm sorry, but my dad won't let me.

If you're worried about people getting angry with you or not liking you

I know you might not like this, but I just can't.

It's hard for me to say this, but no.

You might be disappointed, but I can't.

This may seem weird to you, but I can't do it.

A strong no when you need to make your point

No, that's a really bad idea.

No, I don't want to get in trouble.

No—I just don't want to.

Nope.

No way.

No, and I'm not changing my mind.

QUICK QUIZ

For each of the following situations, find at least one way you could use the No Thanks that is comfortable for you. There are lots of possible ideas. A few answers appear at the bottom of page 17, upside down. (No peeking!)

Situation #1: One of your friends says, "Hey, let's go take that kid's lunch money."

Situation #2: A friend says, "Come on, let's go to the mall," but you don't really feel like it.

Situation #3: Some kids are looking at an Internet site that you know your mom wouldn't want you to look at. Someone says, "Come over here and check this out."

Situation #4: During a test at school, the girl next to you asks if she can see your answers

POSSIBLE RESPONSES

Situation #4: "No, I don't want to get in trouble." "No way!"

Situation #3: "No, I've got to go to go do some other stuff." "No, that's too gross for me." "No, I'll see you guys later."

"No thanks—I'll see you tomorrow."

Situation #2: "Thanks for asking, but I'm going to pass this time." "No, I'm sure it'll be fun, but I can't tonight." "No

Situation #1: "No. That would be mean." "No, just leave him alone." "No. What if someone did that to you?"

Asking Questions

Use Asking Questions when you need information or help.

Telling people how you feel and saying no when you need to are ways to be assertive, like blue jays. Another part of being assertive is asking for what you need, especially when you need help. Blue jays are always willing to squawk for help!

The best way to find things out, or get help, is by Asking Questions. Don't know where the library is? Ask someone. Having trouble with long division? Ask your teacher for help. Not sure why your bike isn't working right? Ask a friend who knows something about bikes. Asking Questions is never dumb.

You may feel embarrassed to ask a question sometimes. What if someone laughs at you? What if someone thinks your question was stupid?

Well, what if someone does? This would be a good time to ask your*self* a question:

What's the **worst** that could happen?

If you find that you are embarrassed about Asking Questions, ask yourself *that* question first. Ask it several times, if you need to. For example, let's say you're having trouble understanding a geography assignment, but you're embarrassed to ask your teacher a question. Here's a conversation you can have with yourself:

"What's the worst that could happen if I ask about the assignment?"

Other kids might laugh at me, or think it's a dumb question.

"What's the worst that could happen if they did laugh or think that?"

I'd be embarrassed.

"What's the worst that could happen if I was embarrassed?"

Well, nothing too bad. And so what? No one's perfect and I'll get over it pretty quick.

The worst that could happen isn't really that bad, when you think about it. Most of the time, other people are glad you asked the question that they were afraid to ask themselves. And, of course, you know what can happen if you *do* ask a question:

- You get an answer.
- You get more information.
- You get the chance to learn and do better.

If you just can't get up the nerve to ask a question when you're in a big group, like a school class, you can always wait until an easier time. For example, you can ask the teacher during recess, when the class is over, or before or after school. Many teachers will let you email them, too.

WAYS TO SAY IT: ASKING QUESTIONS

Excuse me, can you please help me?

Could you please explain that again?

For some reason I'm still not getting it. Could you repeat that?

Could you please go over that again?

I'm sorry to bother you, but can you go through each part?

Tell me again: why did you do it that way?

This is really confusing. Will you please help me?

The Squeaky Wheel

Use the Squeaky Wheel when you need to be persistent.

Using the Power I, the No Thanks, or Asking Questions doesn't work if the person you're talking to doesn't listen. When that happens, you have to be persistent. Being persistent means that you don't give up. It means you repeat what you're saying until the person you're talking to finally understands that you're not giving up. This is especially important when someone is being mean or unfair. Remember, nobody has the right to treat you badly, no matter who they are. You have as much right to feel safe and respected as anyone.

VICTOR had been waiting in line for a long time to get his food in the cafeteria when a bigger kid cut in front of him. "Hey, the line starts back there," Victor said. Victor was

CONTINUED ──▶

proud of himself for standing up to the bigger kid. But the boy just laughed at him, and he didn't go to the end of the line. He was popular, and Victor didn't want to seem like a dork by making a big deal out of it. And he really didn't want to get into an argument or fight. But Victor was upset. It wasn't fair, especially after he had waited so long. He decided to say something again: "Excuse me, please go to the end of the line."

The boy looked at Victor. "All right, kid," he said.

The tool that helps you be persistent is called the Squeaky Wheel. That's what Victor used. Think about it: the squeaky wheel on a bicycle is the wheel that needs attention. It squeaks and squeaks until someone pays attention to it and gives it what it needs. You, too, can continue to "squeak" until someone gives you what you need. The bicycle wheel needs oil. You may need someone to stop teasing you. Or maybe you need someone to give you what belongs to you. Or maybe you need someone to take turns.

Of course, you don't actually squeak (that would get attention you *don't* want!). You talk. You keep repeating what you want in a firm and determined way.

WAYS TO SAY IT: THE SQUEAKY WHEEL

One of your friends starts going through your locker at school and you don't like it.

You: *Hey, quit going through my locker!*

Friend: *I'm checking it out. Don't worry about it.*

You: *No, I'm serious. I don't like it.*

Friend: *Don't have a cow, it's not a big deal.*

You: *Maybe not to you, but I want you to stop it.*

Friend: *Okay, okay, okay!*

It's your turn to use the computer but a girl won't stop using it.

You: *It's my turn to use the computer.*

Girl: *Later.*

You: *No, I've already waited. I need to use it now.*

Girl: *Stop bugging me, I need to finish this.*

You: *I need to do something too, and it's my turn according to the schedule.*

Girl: *Stop bugging me.*

You: *I'll stop bugging you when you let me use the computer. Do I need to get the teacher?*

Girl: *All right, I'm getting off!*

A group of friends wants you to go to a movie, but you don't really want to.

You: *Thanks for inviting me, but I'm just going to hang out at home.*

Friend: *Come on. Don't be such a homebody.*

You: *No, I really don't feel like it.*

Friend: *Why not?*

You: *I just don't want to tonight. I'm tired.*

Friend: *Come on, you can relax in the theater!*

You: *No thanks, I'm staying in tonight.*

Friend: *All right. See you tomorrow.*

You can use the Squeaky Wheel with other tools in this book. In Victor's story, he used the Power I, but it wasn't enough. Then he used the Squeaky Wheel along with the Power I. If they still didn't go, he could have done it again: "Stop cutting in front of me. Go to the end of the line!"

When It's Not Safe to ----- Use the Squeaky Wheel -----

If you're talking to kids who you think might hurt you, don't use the Squeaky Wheel. If you keep talking to kids who are mean, you might not be safe. Instead, don't say anything at all. Just leave right away and find an adult you trust who can help. This is called the Disappearing Act, and you can read about it on pages 69–71.

The tools you learned in this chapter are for being assertive, like a blue jay. When people don't treat you fairly, or respectfully, you can use the tools of the blue jay to get the respect you deserve. Remember that being assertive doesn't mean being mean or tough. You'll have a lot more success getting respect from others if you show it for them, too. Sticking up for yourself can be hard. It takes practice and confidence. But with practice, it gets easier. Soon you'll find that being assertive comes as naturally to you as it does to the blue jay.

Making and Keeping Friends

THE TOOLS OF THE BLACKBIRD

Blackbirds are about the friendliest birds in the world (except when they are protecting babies in their nests, then watch out!). They come together in huge flocks and colonies at different times of the year. If you stand in a field and watch a flock of blackbirds, you can see how much they like to chatter with each other. Blackbird tools make it easier to talk to people and to make and keep friends.

KEVIN didn't do much with other kids. He was shy, and it was embarrassing when he stumbled over words or said the wrong thing. He liked being around people his age but never knew what to say or how to act, so he avoided them.

CONTINUED

That was, until he met Sarah.

How could anyone avoid Sarah? "Hey Kevin, don't you want to play with us?" "How's it going, Kevin?" "Don't you hate math, Kevin?" "Kevin, why don't you eat lunch with us?"

At first, Kevin was nervous about all the attention, and he tried to ignore it. But Sarah didn't give up, and, little by little, he began talking to her. After a while, Sarah became a close friend. And Kevin even learned to start conversations with other people by asking them questions. He could still keep to himself when he wanted to, but he could also be around others and feel more and more comfortable.

Having friends can make school easier and more fun. If you have a friend, you have a person to talk to and enjoy good times with. You also have someone to help you through hard times at school. You can help each other with schoolwork, stick up for each other, and cheer each other up when one of you is down.

But maybe you feel like Kevin. Maybe making friends is hard for you because you're shy or naturally quiet. Even if you're not shy, it can be hard to talk to people you don't know well or who make you feel nervous. The fact is, most people feel shy some of the time, and some feel shy a lot. There's nothing wrong with keeping to yourself when you don't feel like talking.

If you want to have friends, though, you have to be friendly, and that means being kind and thoughtful and learning to talk and listen.

WHEN TO USE THE TOOLS OF THE BLACKBIRD

The tools of the blue jay are for speaking up when you don't like what someone is doing or when you need something. The tools of the blackbird are for speaking up for a more fun reason: to make and keep friends. It *is* hard to talk when you feel shy, quiet, or uncomfortable, but you can do it. Here are a few tips to help you.

8 Ways to Grow More --- Comfortable Around People ---

1. Hang out with kids, even if you don't talk that much.

2. Give people compliments, such as, "I like your T-shirt," or do nice things for them, such as offer some gum or open the door for them.

3. Answer the telephone at home when people call.

4. Do the talking when you go to a store or restaurant.

5. Greet people who come to visit your home.

6. Join a school club, sports team, scout troop, or other group.

7. Do volunteer work that involves people, such as working in the library or at a school event.

8. Ask adults about times when they felt shy, and how they overcame it.

The next thing you can do is practice having conversations. In this chapter, you will learn tools for talking with friends, family, and anyone else you want to talk to. Practice these tools with someone you're comfortable with, such as a good friend, a sister or brother, or a parent. As you talk to more and more people, more and more of the time, it will become easier for you.

The Sherlock Holmes

Use the Sherlock Holmes when you want to start, join, or continue a conversation by asking questions of others.

In the late 1800s and early 1900s, a writer named Sir Arthur Conan Doyle published a series of stories about a very clever detective named Sherlock Holmes. One reason he was so successful was because he asked a lot of questions. When there was a crime, he found out who had been there, when they came, and when they left. He asked all the whos, whats, whys, hows, whens, and wheres. He was very nosy.

When you are having trouble starting or joining a conversation, you can become a Sherlock Holmes. You can ask people about what they've been doing, what they're going to be doing, and what their opinions are. You can ask about their families, their pets, their hobbies, and many other things.

WAYS TO SAY IT: THE SHERLOCK HOLMES

Getting started

What's up?

What have you been doing lately?

What did you do last weekend?

What do you have planned for this week?

What are you doing for the holidays?

What are going to do this summer?

What's there to do around here?

What do you like to do?

Are you going to the dance?

Are you going to the game?

What videos have you seen lately?

What music do you like?

Questions not only start conversations, they keep them going, too. That's because questions force both people in the conversation to talk. You ask the question, and the other person answers it. And once the person answers, you can talk about what the person said. You can even ask another question.

The best questions are open-ended—they can't be answered with a simple yes or no. Yes-or-no questions are *closed* questions. They can end conversations because the answer they ask for is only one word. But open-ended questions invite people to talk more. Consider the difference between the following examples:

Closed Questions	Open-Ended Questions
Was the English test hard?	*What kinds of questions were on the English test?*
Are you in band?	*Why did you choose to learn the trombone?*
Did you watch the show last night?	*What did you think of the show last night?*

Someone could just say yes or no to the closed questions and be done with it. But a person would have to think more about the open-ended questions and give you specific information or opinions in an answer. That would lead to a longer, and better, conversation.

MORE WAYS TO SAY IT: THE SHERLOCK HOLMES

Getting information and opinions

What do you think about (whatever topic you're talking about)?

How do you feel about (a hot topic at school or in the news)?

What's your opinion?

What's your favorite group? Football team? Food? Why?

Who's your favorite teacher? Movie star? Athlete? Singer? Scientist? Why?

When you ask someone questions like these, two of the most important things to remember are to listen really well to the answers and to show you're interested in the person. Check out Chia's story to see what can happen when somebody doesn't pay enough attention to another person's answers.

CHIA was talking a mile a minute about her summer trip to a theme park. "After we saw the parade, we went on the roller coaster. The lines were so-o-o-o long, and we got really hot." Finally, she seemed to remember Shaniqua. "What did you do this summer?" she asked.

"Well, I played in a softball league," Shaniqua said. "It was a lot of fun."

"That's great," Chia said. "Basketball is super fun."

"You mean softball."

"Yeah. Oh! Guess what? We also went on the water ride and the haunted house, which was kind of scary. But it wasn't bad when we got in."

"I'll talk to you later," Shaniqua finally said. "I've got to go do some things before class."

Shaniqua left because Chia wasn't listening to her. Chia asked about Shaniqua's summer, but she didn't pay attention to Shaniqua's answer. Sherlock Holmes wouldn't have been a very good detective if he had just asked questions without paying attention to the answers people gave. His goal was to collect and understand information.

Talking without listening isn't really a conversation at all. It's just exercising your voice and mouth. If you don't listen to the person you're talking to, you aren't likely to make or keep many friends.

Think about how hard you listen when a teacher says, "Pay attention, this is going to be on the test." To be focused, you need to listen to others just the way you would listen to your teacher. Put aside all the other thoughts in your mind (or at least most of them) and concentrate on what the other person is saying. You can show that you're listening by asking more questions and rephrasing what you think the person said. For example, "You felt bad when Jason picked you last to play on his team, huh?" Or, "It sounds like you don't like math very much." It can also help to use short words of encouragement to show that you're listening, such as, "I know what you mean," "I understand," or, "What happened next?" Finally, listen to people's body language, too. If the boy you're talking to says, "I feel fine," but he looks sad, you know that he really isn't fine. You can ask him more about his feelings.

MORE WAYS TO SAY IT: THE SHERLOCK HOLMES

Other fun questions

What Internet sites do you go to?

What foods can you cook?

What do you want to be when you grow up?

If you had a million dollars, what would you do with it?

Where would you most like to go for a vacation?

Who is your favorite baseball player? Soccer player? Comedian?

Once you get in the habit, it will become easier to think of good questions and easier to talk to people.

Tool #6

Sharing

Use Sharing when you want to start, join, or continue conversations by telling others about yourself.

Another way to start conversations and keep them going is to tell others something about yourself. Other kids are more likely to talk about themselves if you share something about yourself. Sharing means telling others your opinions, interests, plans, and feelings.

Sometimes you use Sharing to start a conversation. Other times kids might tell you something about themselves first. Then, you use Sharing to add to the subject and keep the conversation going. For example, if a kid says, "I don't like it when it's foggy like this," you can say, "I don't like it very much either. My favorite weather is a clear day right after a snow storm." Or if a friend says, "I like to play cards," you can say, "Me too, but I'm better at chess. Do you play chess?"

When you're sharing about yourself, it's important to be honest and sincere. Don't exaggerate or lie. The point of Sharing is to tell other people things about yourself—real things—so they can get to know you. You want to do this in a relaxed, friendly way—not by bragging, showing off, or talking too much about yourself.

You can also use Sharing along with the Sherlock Holmes. You can share something about yourself, then ask follow-up questions to find out about the person you're talking to. In the following examples, notice how Sharing sometimes seems to work naturally with the Sherlock Holmes.

WAYS TO SAY IT: SHARING

Starting conversations

I feel a little shy in these situations. How about you?

Are you new in this class? I am, too, and I'm a little nervous.

This isn't too bad for cafeteria food. How's yours?

I'm having trouble with this computer program. Did you have any problems with it?

I don't really like math that much, but I do like English. What's your favorite subject?

That was a great football game last night. Do you think we have a shot at the playoffs?

Keeping a conversation going

When a friend tells you about a time she was in a play: *You were brave to be in a play like that. I think I would be scared in front of all those people.*

When someone says that he went to a national park over the vacation: *I've never been there, but I'd love to go. What did you do there?*

When someone mentions she had two tests in one day: *Yikes, I wouldn't like that! What were they on?*

When a friend tells you about his swimming team practice: *Wow—I don't know if I could swim that long and fast. Don't you get super tired?*

As with the Sherlock Holmes, you don't have to use Sharing if you don't want to. But, besides just helping with conversations, Sharing can help keep a friendship healthy. When you share about yourself, people learn to trust you and like you. Also, if a friendship becomes one-way—with only one person doing most of the Sharing—that friendship is one-sided and not healthy. It probably won't last because the friend who is doing all the Sharing may feel like the other person isn't interested in the friendship.

TooL #7

Kind Talk

Use Kind Talk when you want to show others you respect them and care about them.

You know that being polite means saying things like please, thank you, and excuse me. It also means showing respect and treating people the same way that you'd like to be treated. Nobody likes to be bossed around. Sometimes you may need to be assertive, and sometimes you may even need to speak to people in a strong voice to stop them from doing something harmful. But even then you can be polite. Polite, respectful talk is one kind of Kind Talk.

But Kind Talk is more than just being polite. Kind Talk is going out of your way to help others through your words. It means giving words of support to people who are lonely or sad and giving sincere compliments to others. Use Kind Talk to make new friends and show the friends you have that you care about them.

WAYS TO SAY IT: KIND TALK

Being polite

You want an adult to pick you up from school.
You: *Could you please pick me up from school?*

You're brother is watching TV and you want to watch something different.
You: *When your show ends, can I please choose a show?*

Somebody picks up a book you drop and gives it to you.
You: *Thanks.*

Your teacher helps you with a homework problem.
You: *Thanks for helping me.*

You need to get past somebody who is standing in the doorway.
You: *Excuse me, I'm coming through.*

Giving compliments

Your friend gets an A on her test.
You: *Wow, nice work.*

Your team loses the baseball game, and you see the other team's pitcher in the parking lot.
You: *Hey, great game. You had some wicked stuff out there.*

Your aunt makes a tasty dinner.
You: *That was delicious. Thanks.*

Your stepbrother gets a new haircut.
You: *Looking good, bro.*

Giving support

A new kid at school is standing all alone and looks bashful.
You: *Hi, my name is _____. You're new, right? Where are you from?*

A kindergarten kid is being teased by some first graders.
You: *Hey, leave him alone. He's hanging out with me.*

A kid on the playground twists her ankle and is sitting in pain.

You: *Are you all right? I think you need some ice on that. I'll go get some help.*

Your team beats another team in soccer, and you see one of the other players.

You: *You have a good team. That was a tough game.*

Kind Talk is adding kindness to somebody's life with your words. But you know what? It can be even more than that. It can also be adding kindness through your actions, by doing favors for others.

MORE WAYS TO SAY IT: KIND TALK

Doing favors

A girl in the cafeteria has spilled her milk and is wiping it up with a napkin.

You: *I can help. I've got another napkin.*

One of your friends is making a special trip to drop a book off at the library.
You: *I'm going to the library to study. I'll drop it off for you.*

Your grandma starts to take the garbage out.
You: *Wait, Gram, let me do that for you.*

Your sister can't find her backpack.
You: *I'll help you look for it.*

Your dad is carrying in the groceries.
You: *Hey, Dad, I'll grab the rest.*

 # Practice Time

Together with a friend or family adult, practice starting and continuing conversations using all the tools in this chapter together. Here's how:

1. **Decide on a topic.** Figure out what you'd like to talk about—for example, comic books.

2. **Sherlock Holmes.** Think of one or two questions you could ask the other person. If the subject is comic books, you could ask, "What's your favorite comic? Who is your favorite character? Why?"

3. **Sharing.** Think of one or two things about yourself that you can share on the subject. For example, you might share who your favorite author is, what your favorite comic book is, or what kind of comic books you like.

4. **Kind Talk.** Think of a couple kind things you could do or say. With the comic books example, you might offer to let

the person borrow a favorite book of yours, or you might compliment the person on his or her collection.

5. Put it all together. Choose one of the items from your list, such as a question, and start a conversation with your partner. If you get stuck for more to say, look back to your list and choose something else to say—perhaps sharing something about yourself.

Practice several conversations with your partner. All conversations don't have to include all three tools. But practicing them all will make you more comfortable talking to others. ■

Maybe you'd like to be just like a blackbird and hang out and chatter with huge flocks of friends. Or maybe you prefer to have a few different friends for different activities. Or maybe you'd rather have just one or two really close friends. Whatever you're comfortable with, the tools of the blackbird can help you get along in lots of social situations.

Ending Arguments and Fights

THE TOOLS OF THE DOVE

Doves spend much of their time perched in the shade, cooing softly. A dove's voice is one of the most soothing sounds in nature. For thousands of years, the dove has been a symbol of peace to people all over the world. To the ancient Greeks, it stood for love. In ancient Japan, a dove carrying a sword symbolized the end of war. You can use dove tools to smooth ruffled feathers and settle conflicts.

Even if you're good at making and keeping friends, it still can be hard to get along with people all the time. Have you ever argued with someone at school over something like whose turn it is to use the hall pass or sharing somebody's handheld video game? Have you ever argued with your family over doing chores or homework? Sometimes even the best of friends fight or argue. Fighting and arguing are forms of conflict, and conflict is impossible to avoid at times.

Sometimes conflicts are over something small, like when you and a friend can't agree on which show to watch or who gets the last piece of cake. Sometimes conflict seems bigger, like when people have strong and differing opinions about what happened in a game or how to do a group project. Conflict can occcur when people don't treat each other fairly or when they don't follow rules. There are many ways that conflict can arise.

However it happens, conflict isn't fun. If you're not getting along with your best friend, it feels lousy. Even a conflict with someone you don't know very well can make you feel angry, sad, or scared. And some conflict can cause a lot of damage and pain. If a conflict is very big or lasts very long, it can be terrible.

One way to avoid conflict is simple: by listening to people. When you listen you show respect for others. It also helps you understand what they want or need. Think about how frustrating it is when others don't listen to you. When people don't listen to each other, it can cause conflict—or make conflict bigger.

JAMEL AND LATISHA'S teams were playing dodgeball at school. Each team had just two people left in the circle. Jamel threw the ball hard and he thought it just tipped Latisha's hand. "You're out!" he called.

CONTINUED ⟶

"Just missed me," Latisha said.
"No way," Jamel argued. "It hit your hand."
"No, it didn't. I would have felt it."
"You guys are cheaters!"
"Baby!"
"Let's go, guys," Jamel called out to his team. "They're a bunch of cheaters."

You can avoid many conflicts if you don't let yourself argue over things that aren't worth it. Some things—like protecting yourself or others, or saying no when you need to—are definitely worth fighting for. But it often doesn't make sense to argue over something like Jamel and Latisha's dodgeball game—or who won the swimming race, or who is better at math, or what middle school is cooler, or whose turn it is to take out the garbage, or who has the best skateboard. Many big fights get started by disagreements over small things. Don't let that happen to you. Think about how important the argument is. If you think you can let it go, give it a try.

WHEN TO USE THE TOOLS OF THE DOVE

If a conflict does arise—and you want it to end—at least one person has to step up to resolve (end) it. Conflicts don't resolve themselves. It takes a leader. In Jamel and Latisha's story, either kid could have realized that a dodgeball game isn't important enough to fight over. Latisha could have said, "I don't think you got me, but if you think you did, I'll step out." Or Jamel could have said, "I guess I could have been wrong. I'll get you for sure next time." Either way, they would have kept playing the game, and their tempers would have stayed cool. The conflict would have stopped.

You can choose to be a leader and resolve conflicts. The tools of the dove can help you.

TooL #8

The Coin Toss

Use the Coin Toss when you want to quickly resolve
a small conflict before it gets big.

Some conflicts start out small. If nobody wants to step up to solve a conflict, even a tiny one, it can grow—and get ugly. It's best to find quick and fair ways to solve small conflicts right away.

Disagreements over things like taking turns or sharing can be solved by simply tossing a coin. You've probably used this tool before. If you've ever watched the start of a football game, you've probably seen it. The referee tosses a coin into the air to decide which team receives the ball first.

Say you and a friend are starting to argue about who will give their speech first when you get to class. One of you can toss a coin in the air while the other calls out heads or tails. Let the coin land on the ground and then see which side is facing up. If the caller chose the side that ended face up, he or she gets to go first (or last, if that's what you were arguing over!).

WAYS TO DO IT: THE COIN TOSS

You and someone else want to use the same computer at the same time at school.
You: *Let's split the class time in half. We'll flip to see who goes first.*

There are two chores to be done at home—washing the dishes and doing the laundry—and neither you nor your brother wants to do them.

You: *We'll toss a coin and the winner can choose which chore to do.*

Somebody at your home needs to take out the garbage, but nobody can remember whose turn it is.

You: *We'll toss a coin and the loser takes his or her turn now.*

You can get the same kinds of solutions in other simple ways. You could have a third person write down a number between one and ten. You could draw straws or play rock, paper, scissors.

Solution Time

*Use Solution Time when you want to resolve
a large or important conflict.*

If your conflict is too big or important for the Coin Toss, try Solution Time. Solution Time is a time-out from fighting and a time-in to making solutions. Solutions are ways of solving problems, or conflicts.

The first and most important thing you have to do in Solution Time is CHOOSE TO SOLVE THE CONFLICT. Someone has to take the first step to end the conflict. Sometimes it's hard to be the person who steps up to find a solution, because your feelings during a conflict can be really strong. But don't let your emotions get the best of you. Be the one who is willing to suggest a solution.

For example, imagine that you're at school and your group gets into an argument with another group about using the volleyball court. Before tempers start to fly, you can take control. Say, "Hold on, let's think for a second. Maybe we can come up with a solution. How about playing against each other?"

WIN-WIN

For a solution to work, it has to work for both sides. Both sides need to win something, which is called *win-win*. If your solution only benefits you, it's not going to make the other person very happy. If one person isn't happy, the conflict will go on. Read on to see what happened to Alicia when she had a conflict with a friend.

ALICIA and Maria were working on their art projects. "Could you please hand me the light-blue paint?" asked Maria.

CONTINUED ———→

"Sure," said Alicia, "but there's just a little bit left, so don't use it all."

"I need to use it all," said Maria. "Otherwise, I won't be able to finish the sky in my picture."

"But I need some, too."

"I'm sorry, but I asked for it first and I'm going to use as much as I need."

"That's not fair," said Alicia. "We need a better solution."

"That is the solution," said Maria. "You need to find your own paint."

Do you think that Alicia believed this was a good solution in her conflict with Maria? Chances are she didn't. Let's consider another example. Imagine you and your sister want the same ice cream sandwich. If your solution is that you get to eat it all no matter what, your sister is going to fight the solution. She probably feels that she has as much right to win the conflict as you do. Neither one of you will be happy unless you each win something. With the ice cream sandwich, you could split it so you each get half. Or you could buy another ice cream sandwich, so you both have one. In either case, you both get what you want (win-win).

Sometimes you can't get everything you want, like a whole ice cream sandwich. In that case, you can compromise. That means you both give up something so that you both can win something. When you split the ice cream sandwich with your sister, you are compromising. You both would rather have a whole one. But sharing the one you have is

easier than going to the store for another one. By splitting the treat, you both give up something (half an ice cream sandwich) and you both get something (half an ice cream sandwich). You both win.

---- Steps to Solution Time ----

1. Choose to resolve the conflict.

2. Define the problem. What exactly is the conflict and what do you want to happen? What does the other person want?

3. Think of some win-win solutions and suggest them to the other person. Ask for the other person's ideas, too.

4. Choose a win-win solution with the other person, and act on it.

WAYS TO DO IT: SOLUTION TIME

Following are some conflict situations, along with suggestions for the four steps to Solution Time. Can you think of other solutions?

Situation: Everyone in your class has to do an oral report on a U.S. president. You and another student both want to do your reports on Abraham Lincoln.

Solution Time:

1. Choose to resolve the conflict: Say, "Maybe there's a way we can both get what we want. Let's try to figure it out."

2. Define the problem: You both want to do your report on the same president.

3. Possible solutions:

- Do your report together, if the teacher will let you.
- Ask the teacher if you can split up his presidency—one of you does the early years, one does the later years.
- You both do Lincoln.

4. Choose a solution and do it.

Situation: A friend is angry at you because he thinks you told lies about him (but you didn't). He doesn't believe you when you tell him you didn't, and that makes you angry, too. You start yelling at each other.

Solution Time:

1. Choose to resolve the conflict: Calm down and say, "I understand why you would be mad if someone was lying about you, but let's see if we can figure out a solution without fighting."

2. Define the problem: Your friend thinks you were telling lies about him and he feels angry. You want him to know you didn't tell lies about him. It makes you angry that he doesn't believe you.

3. Possible solutions:

- Walk away and call him on the phone later that night to talk about it, after you both have a chance to calm down.
- Offer to find out how the lies got started.
- Ask a teacher or parent to help you find out what happened.

4. Choose a solution and do it.

Situation: Your mom doesn't want you to pierce your ears.

Solution Time:

1. Choose to resolve the conflict: Say, "Mom, can we talk about a solution to this disagreement that works for both of us?"

2. Define the problem: You want to pierce your ears, but your mom doesn't want you to.

3. Possible solutions:

- Agree on a certain age when you can choose for yourself.

- You both go to a doctor or pierced ear shop to talk about ear piercing.

- You can wear "pierced-look" earrings.

4. Choose a solution and do it.

 ## Practice Time

Think of a conflict you've had with someone recently. For example, maybe you argued with your brother over cleaning the bedroom you share or fought with a friend over what music to listen to. Write down as many solutions as you can think of for the conflict, making sure each solution is win-win for you and the other person. By thinking about solutions to problems you've already had, you'll become better at finding solutions to new conflicts. ■

REFEREE

Sometimes you have a conflict with somebody who has no interest in finding a win-win solution. Sometimes people just want their own way and don't care about compromising. If you can't work out a fair, win-win solution to your conflict, you can bring in a referee to help you. The referee listens to both sides of the conflict and decides on a solution. This sometimes happens in the adult world. If two adults can't compromise on a problem, they take their problem to a mediator or judge in a court of law. Mediators and judges are kinds of referees.

If you find that you cannot reach a win-win solution with someone, ask a parent, teacher, or other adult to be a referee. (Some schools even train kids to be referees, or peer mediators.) Then, explain your side of the conflict to the referee. Let the person you're in conflict with explain his or her side, too. Then explain what you want to happen to resolve the conflict. After listening, the referee will come up with a solution or two.

TooL #10

The CooL Down

Use the Cool Down when you want to get away from a conflict and take control of strong, angry feelings.

Did you know that scientists have found that our feelings are faster than our thoughts? This is usually a good thing, because it means our bodies can respond to danger very quickly. If you're afraid of snakes and one slithers up next to you, your feelings of fear will make you immediately jerk away without even thinking about it. Unfortunately, this also happens when your goofy buddy dangles a rubber snake down the back of your shirt. And if somebody says something mean you, your feelings of anger will make you immediately want to say something mean back.

That's the problem with our quick and strong feelings: they can get us into conflict before our more cool, logical thoughts can calm us down. When you're in a big fight or argument, and your feelings are intense—or hot—it's hard to think clearly and fairly. It's hard to take control of your hot feelings and make the choice to solve the conflict. When that's the case, you may need to do the Cool Down.

The Cool Down means you choose to stop arguing and get away from the person you're arguing with. You take a walk around the block, shoot baskets, read a book, draw a picture, write about your feelings—or do just about anything else to calm yourself—instead of fighting. After a while, your feelings will cool down. Then you'll have a more clear head to think about solutions to your conflict.

WAYS TO DO IT: THE COOL DOWN

Here is a list of twenty ways to Cool Down. Which ones work best for you? Can you think of others?

1. Go for a run.

2. Listen to your favorite band or song.

3. Eat a banana (seriously!).

4. Ride your bike or skateboard, or go in-line skating.

5. Write a poem or rap.

6. Do your homework.

7. Help your brother or sister with his or her homework.

8. Call, email, or instant message a friend (but don't say mean things about the person you're in conflict with).

9. Check out your favorite blog or Web site.

10. Read a book.

11. Play a game of solitaire.

12. Vacuum.

13. Climb the monkey bars.

14. Take a nap.

15. Take a bath.

16. Sing a song in the shower.

17. Make a painting or drawing.

18. Take the dog for a walk.

19. Climb a tree.

20. Look at old photos of your family.

As with Solution Time, the Cool Down requires that you be a leader. You have to step up and take charge of your feelings. If you let hot feelings be in charge, you might end up in a fight, or saying or doing something that really hurts the other person. You might ruin a good friendship. It's a lot better to Cool Down when you're too hot to talk.

If you show respect for others you can prevent many conflicts, but sometimes conflict is unavoidable. For those times, remember the tools of the dove. Remember to be a leader with yourself, a person who will act to end conflicts.

Stopping Teasing and Bullying

THE TOOLS OF THE HUMMINGBIRD

Hummingbirds are the smallest birds in the world, but they're also the bravest. They've been known to protect themselves and their young when dogs, cats, hawks, or even humans invade their territory. The hummingbird sets a good example to follow when dealing with teasers and bullies—even if they're bigger than you.

Let's face it, every person on this planet has been teased. Sometimes teasing is meant to be playful and fun, like when family members kid you because you like pickles on your pizza. Other times it's meant to be mean, like when a kid at school tries to make you feel bad for the clothes you wear.

Bullying is more than teasing. Bullying is when people actually try to hurt other people—with their words or with their bodies. All these things are bullying:

- mean teasing
- gossip
- put-downs
- hitting
- pushing
- ripping up or tossing kids' papers or books
- making threats

All these kinds of bullying are forms of conflict. But you probably won't be able to end these conflicts with the Coin Toss, Solution Time, or even the Cool Down. That's because people who bully or tease usually aren't interested in solving conflicts. They want to start one. There is no win-win solution, because the bully thinks the only way to win is by hurting someone. For the person being hurt, the only way to win is by ending the bullying.

Every time **GONZALO** went onto the playground, a group of boys from his class picked on him. When he heard them yell, "Hey shorty, get over here," he knew it was starting again. They did things like tip his ball cap and push him down. They called him "teacher's pet," and once they made him push a penny across the ground with his nose.

Gonzalo loved to play soccer with his friends. But now he avoided the playground whenever he could. He stayed in the cafeteria all during lunch and he hid in the bathroom at

CONTINUED ——→

recess. Sometimes he even pretended to be sick so he could stay home from school. The boys said if he told a teacher about what they were doing to him he would get it even worse. Gonzalo felt miserable, but he didn't know what to do.

What happened to Gonzalo was not his fault. He didn't ask to be bullied, and he didn't do anything to deserve it. If someone bullies you, it's not your fault, either, and you don't deserve it. Bullying can be painful, and nobody should have to put up with it. Nobody has the right to hurt, scare, or embarrass you at school, on the bus, or anywhere else—even at home.

But bullying happens a lot. People who bully usually want to feel control and power. Some bullies want others to feel pain because they think it shows how strong they are. Some think it's funny to make others cry or act scared. Many people who bully have been taught that bullying is the best way to get what they want. They've been taught that might makes right. Many have been bullied at home, and they end up feeling angry. Anger is hard to keep inside. It has to come out, and bullies end up taking it out on others.

Whatever the reasons are, it's not fair or right for anyone to bully someone else. Nobody should have to feel the way Gonzalo did. If someone bullies you, you have the power to end it. One thing you can do is use your words and body language to make the bully stop. You'll learn tools to help you do that in this chapter. If you practice and use the tools, you'll be able to stop more bullying situations. You'll be able to deal with bullying more often and with more confidence. But when these tools don't solve the problem, **get help from an adult.** Doing this *isn't* tattling.

---- Telling Is Not Tattling ----

People who bully love when their victims don't tell anyone about the bullying, because they don't want to get in trouble. If no adult finds out about the bullying, bullies stay in control of the situation. Control is what bullies want.

Sometimes kids are afraid to tell on someone who's bullying them. They don't want people to think they're tattling, or being "sissies," or they're afraid that the bullying will get even worse if they tell. Don't believe it. The bullying can get worse if you *don't* tell.

You have the right to go to school and not be bullied. That right is guaranteed by laws or rules in most communities. Schools should provide a safe place to learn. That means no bullying. If you or others are being bullied by someone, talk to an adult— a parent, teacher, principal, or somebody else you trust—in private. If you're afraid that the bullying will get worse, tell the adult that, too. Ask the adult for the privacy and protection you need. Telling on a bully isn't tattling, it's standing up for your rights and the rights of others.

AVOIDING BULLYING

One way to stop bullying is to keep it from happening in the first place. And one way to do that is to act confident. Bullies usually choose victims who look shy or unsure of themselves. That's because those people seem less likely to stand up for themselves. To look sure and confident:

- Stand up straight.
- Hold your head high.
- Look the bully in the eye.
- Speak with a firm voice.

If you don't look scared, you won't look like a target for bullying.

Another thing that helps is to stay around friends and other people. Bullies like to pick on people who are alone. You don't need to be best friends with everyone, but hang out with other kids whenever you can.

The best way to make and keep friends is to be *friendly.* If you're shy about making friends, check out the the blackbird tools (pages 24–39) for some tips to help you.

WHEN TO USE THE TOOLS OF THE HUMMINGBIRD

You know that bullies want to have power and control over their victims. The main way they get that is by causing people to cry, get mad, or feel afraid. So how can you get people to leave you alone once they've started bullying you? Don't give them the power they want. Don't let them control you by making you do any of those things.

Even if you feel upset, try not to show it. Don't cry or attack the person who's bullying you. Make it clear that only *you* are in control of you. If bullies can't make you react the way they want you to, they'll get tired of trying. They'll figure out that you're not an easy target. The tools of the hummingbird can help you.

TooL #11

The Power I for Teasing

Use the Power I for Teasing when you want to tell someone that you don't like his or her teasing.

Remember the blue jay tool called the Power I (pages 9–12)? It can be a hummingbird tool, too. The first thing you should do if you are teased is use a Power I to tell the person to stop: "Please stop that," or, "Quit it!" Often, the teaser was just trying to have fun and didn't know the teasing was hurting you. If that's the case, asking the person to stop will usually do the trick. If it doesn't, you can use a stronger Power I: "I asked you to stop and I want you to cut it out now!" You can also use a strong question, like, "Why are you doing that after I asked you to stop?"

Remember, your body language and tone of voice when using the Power I are important. Stand tall, look the person in the eye, and don't move away. Speak in a clear and steady voice. Don't act threatening or mean, but do be honest and direct. Just walk away when you're finished.

Please knock it off!

Practice Time

Practice speaking in a firm voice on your own. Practice with a friend, too. Then practice with a family adult. You will surprise teasers when they see that you can be firm when you need to be. ∎

WAYS TO SAY IT: POWER I FOR TEASING

I want you to knock it off.

I don't like that. Please stop.

Stop annoying me.

Stop it!

Cut it out!

The Shrug

Use the Shrug when you want to show people that their teasing doesn't bother you.

One quick, easy, and effective way of dealing with teasing is to shrug it off. With the Shrug, you show teasers that you don't care about their words. You don't pay any attention to them— you look away, walk away, act bored, and smile or laugh if you want. It might help to say something like "who cares?" or "so what?" You give the person who's teasing you as little attention as possible.

Great Athletes
------- Who Do the Shrug -------

If you ever watch sports on TV, you'll see great athletes who do the Shrug very well. Most people think Michael Jordan was the best basketball player of all time. He was also very good at the Shrug. Other athletes would trash talk him, or tease him, trying to rattle his concentration. But Jordan would just smile and jog away. Sometimes he would even laugh. He never let other people's comments distract him from the game.

Once again, your body language is important. With the Power I you look the teasers straight in the eyes, but with the Shrug you don't look at them at all. You look beyond them and you don't talk to them. The point is to show teasers that their comments don't matter to you.

The Mighty Might

*Use the Mighty Might when you want to end teasing
by giving a teaser nothing to say.*

A more direct way to deal with teasing is to take control of the conversation away from the person who's teasing you. Teasers want you to react to their words with fear or pain. The Mighty Might gives them a reaction they don't expect and leaves them with little else to say. And that takes the fun out of teasing.

With the Mighty Might, you don't agree *or* disagree with teasers. Instead, you say phrases like "you might be right" or "I might." You don't get into an argument. You don't get mad or scared. You simply leave no place for the conversation to go. There's nothing left for teasers to say.

WAYS TO SAY IT: THE MIGHTY MIGHT

Teaser: *You don't know how to spell.*
You: *You might be right.*

Teaser: *Your clothes are ugly.*
You: *You might be right.*
Teaser: *I am right, did you get that shirt at a garage sale?*
You: *You might be right.*

You don't have to say *might* with the Mighty Might. You can also use other phrases that do the same thing, such as "could be" or "maybe."

MORE WAYS TO SAY IT: THE MIGHTY MIGHT

Teaser: *You sure are skinny, Scarecrow!*
You: *Maybe.*

Teaser: *What are you—stupid?*
You: *Could be.*

Teaser: *Hey punk, nice wheelchair. Don't you know how to walk?*
You: *Maybe not.*
Teaser: *You're so lame.*
You: *Maybe.*

The Mighty Might leaves you with nothing more to say, just like the teaser. So after you've used two or three Mighty Mights, just ignore teasers. You've made your point: teasers now know that you are not a fun target for teasing.

The Comeback Kid

Use the Comeback Kid when you want a strong way to respond to teasing.

What if you use a Power I to tell a teaser to stop, but it doesn't work? What if you can't shrug off a teaser? What if the Mighty Might doesn't feel right, because you want to strongly disagree with what a teaser is saying?

If you feel you need something stronger to take control away from a teaser, you can use a comeback. A comeback is a smart or funny response to teasing. You use it to show that you're not going to give in to teasing and that teasing you isn't fun or easy. You take control of your half of the conversation.

A comeback can be assertive or funny, but it should not be mean or threatening. One of the worst things that could happen is to let someone else's bullying turn you into a bully yourself. Don't let someone do that to you. You'll have more respect for yourself if you don't get mean or violent. Other people will have more respect for you, too.

A word of warning: With comebacks, it's important to remember not to push things too far. If you feel like the conversation is getting too hot, loud, or angry, it's time to stop talking and walk away. Is the person clenching a fist? Is the person breathing hard or getting bug-eyed? If so, it's time for you to get out of there. If you know a certain person is dangerous before he or she even starts bothering you, don't try a comeback. In these situations, your best bet is to get help from an adult as fast as you can.

There are three ways of using the Comeback Kid: the Power You, the Complete Denial, and the I Can't Hear You.

COMEBACK KID #1: THE POWER YOU

Kids who tease you are making you the target of their mean words. They are trying to make you feel bad by putting attention on you. The Power You puts the attention back on a teaser. The rule of the Power You is to respond to teasing with "you" statements about the teaser. Use the words *you* or *your* to point out why the teasing is wrong, and then walk away. Again, you don't want to be mean, but you should be honest and direct.

WAYS TO SAY IT: THE POWER YOU

Teaser: *You talk funny. What's your problem?*
You: *Everybody seems to understand me except for you.*

Teaser: *Hey, great hair. You look like a goof.*
You: *My hair is none of your business. Besides, I like it this way.*

Be aware of your tone of voice and body language when using the Power You. If you put too much oomph on the "you," other people might take it the wrong way. They might think you are being mean or starting a fight. Here are some examples of smart ways and not-so-smart ways to use the Power You.

NOT-SO-SMART WAY   **SMART WAY**

Here are some more ways to use the Power You. As you read them, think about the right body language and tone of voice.

Teaser: *You stink at baseball.*
You: *Maybe you know someone who's perfect at baseball.*
I know I don't.

Teaser: *What a huge butt you have!*
You: *Why are you so interested in my butt? Anyway, I could care less what you think.*

Teaser: *Four eyes, four eyes!*
You: *Are you serious? You've never seen people wearing glasses before?*

 Practice Time

Start practicing the Comeback Kid tools in your mind as you read them. Then practice out loud in front of a mirror. (When practicing out loud, practice your body language and tone of voice as well.) Finally, practice with someone, such as a family grown-up, a brother or sister, or a good friend. Have the person do the teasing so you can practice responding to the mean words. Then, you pretend to tease and have the other person respond to your mean words. This gives you the chance to see what responses would be hardest for a teaser to deal with. ■

COMEBACK KID #2: COMPLETE DENIAL

Complete Denial is disagreeing with every single thing teasers say. For example, if somebody says you have freckles, you  say, "No I don't" (even if you do have freckles). If a teaser says you have a funny-looking nose, you say, "No I don't." Even if a teaser says the sky is blue, you say, "No it's not." After a few Complete Denials, teasers will usually get tired of trying to make you upset, and they'll stop. If they don't, just ignore them or walk away. You've made your point that you're not a fun and easy target. They'll get the same Complete Denial every time.

WAYS TO SAY IT: COMPLETE DENIAL

Teaser: *You play like a baby.*
You: *No I don't.*

Teaser: *You walk like a geek.*
You: *No I don't.*
Teaser: *Yes you do, check out the mirror.*
You: *No I don't.*

Teaser: *Don't you ever take a bath? You smell.*
You: *No I don't.*
Teaser: *P.U., just smell it.*
You: *No I don't.*

Sometimes, using Complete Denial means saying yes to what a teaser says.

Teaser: *You're out! Ha ha! You can't play kickball at all.*
You: *Yes I can.*

COMEBACK KID #3: I CAN'T HEAR YOU

With I Can't Hear You, you pretend you can't hear what teasers are saying. You respond to every tease with something like, "I can't hear you." As with all the Comeback Kid tools, it only takes a few times to make it clear that you're not giving in to the teasing. You don't want this to become an argument, shouting match, or fight. After you do it a few times, just walk away or ignore the teasers. You've shown that you're not going to be an easy target for them—now, or in the future.

WAYS TO SAY IT: I CAN'T HEAR YOU

Teaser: *When you sit down, the whole room shakes.*
You: *I can't hear you.*
Teaser: *I said you're fat.*
You: *Sorry, can't hear you. Hopefully you said something nice.*

Teaser: *You think you're so smart, don't you?*
You: *I'm sorry, I didn't hear what you said.*
Teaser: *You're a nerd.*
You: *Sorry. I can't hear what you're saying. Maybe we can talk another day.*

Teaser: *Hey, Bucky the Beaver, nice buck teeth.*
You: *I'm sorry, did you say something?*
Teaser: *Yeah, I said nice teeth, Bucky.*
You: *I can't hear you. Talk to me some other time.*

WHAT IF YOU'RE THE ONE DOING THE BULLYING?

The tools in this chapter can help you if someone bullies you. But people who bully also need help. If you think you're becoming a bully, you can change. The first step is CHOOSING to change. Then, apologize to people you've bullied or teased. Try to make up for the mean things you've done. Two ways to do that are to invite kids you've bullied to play with you or to stick up for them when someone else picks on them. Doing those things will make you feel a lot better about yourself. If you need help, ask an adult. Parents, teachers, and principals are good people to talk to about bullying. Also, your school may have a counselor or psychologist who is trained to help kids with problems like bullying. They can help bullies learn to respect themselves and others.

TooL #15

The Disappearing Act

Use the Disappearing Act when you might be in danger and you need to get away.

Most of the time, the Power I, the Shrug, the Mighty Might, or one of the Comeback Kid tools will work to end teasing and nonviolent bullying. But what should you do if the tools don't work? When that happens, get away from the bully and tell a teacher or other adult. This is called the Disappearing Act.

Another time to use the Disappearing Act is when bullying or another situation gets dangerous. It's usually pretty easy to tell when you're in a dangerous situation. Trust what your feelings are telling you. If a group of kids surrounds you or pushes you around on the playground, that's dangerous. If someone says, "I'm going to teach you a lesson you'll never forget," that's dangerous. If a mean-looking group starts to move toward you in the locker room, that's dangerous. If you see a bully carrying a weapon, like a bat or knife, that's *really* dangerous.

If you ever find yourself in one of these situations, or any other dangerous situation, disappear. Take your friends with you and get to a safe place—such as the principal's office, your teacher's classroom, or your home—as soon as possible. You can talk to a teacher or parent about other safe places to go. Whatever place you choose, try to make it a place where there are adults who can help you. When you get there, tell the adults about the problem and ask for their help.

-------- McGruff House® --------

McGruff the Crime Dog®

One place to run to is a McGruff House. These are safe houses especially for kids who are bullied, followed, or hurt while walking in a neighborhood. You can tell a McGruff House because it will have a picture of McGruff the Crime Dog® and the words *McGruff House* in a window or on a door. For more information, refer to www.mcgruff.org.

If you can't get away before somebody physically attacks you, you have the right to defend yourself. If you have to, fight to keep the attacker off of you. Call out for help if you can, or have others run for help.

The Disappearing Act is the most important tool of the hummingbird. Even hummingbirds, as brave as they are, know when to get away. You, too, need to know when to get away.

---- A Word About Strangers ----

Also use the Disappearing Act when you're approached by a stranger and you don't feel safe or comfortable. Always run away from strangers who try to get you in their car or try to get you to go somewhere with them. Don't believe them if they say that your mom or dad told them to pick you up. If they try to grab you, fight and scream for help as strongly and loudly as you can and run away. Even if a stranger doesn't talk to you or grab you but you feel uncomfortable, get away. And make sure to immediately report the stranger's actions to your teacher or another adult that you know and trust.

One final note about teasing and bullying: it's up to every kid to make school safe and fun. That includes people who are not bullied but see it at school. The tools of the hummingbird help you take care of yourself, but if you see others being bullied, you can help them, too. Walk up to the bully and say, "Hey, leave him alone." If you can, bring your friends: "She's with us, so back off." You can discourage bullying by inviting kids who are alone to hang out with you and your friends. That way they don't become easy targets. Bullies think bullying is cool, and if you stand up to them with friends, you show them that it's not cool and it's not okay.

Dealing with Blame

THE TOOLS OF THE CROW

Farmers sometimes blame crows for destroying crops. Crows deserve some of this blame. They love to eat corn and some other crops. But crows don't deserve all the blame, because they also eat bugs and other pests that harm many crops.

Crows are among the smartest of all birds. They have strong memories and are good at learning from their experiences. The tools of the crow can help you learn from experiences and deal with blame.

One nice thing about being a human being is that you have the power to make choices about many parts of your life. You can't choose how tall you are, how fast you can run, whether you have to wear braces, or whether you have a big nose or small toes. But you can choose to treat your body well by eating a healthy diet, getting exercise and rest, and not smoking or using drugs. And you can choose to respect yourself and others by being kind instead of mean, by being honest instead of stealing and cheating, and by putting your best effort into school. You have a wonderful power within you to make good decisions.

Of course, sometimes you make bad choices—everyone does. Nobody's perfect. For example, you might choose not to study for a test and then do poorly on it. You might lose your temper and say mean things to a friend. You might choose to play catch too close to a neighbor's house and then break a window with the ball. You might choose to tell a lie about who did it.

But even if you make a wrong choice, you still have another choice to make. This one is very important. You can choose how to deal with your decision. You can choose to say it was someone else's fault. You can choose to act like it didn't happen. Or you can choose to take responsibility for your mistake.

Taking responsibility for poor choices and mistakes means admitting to them, apologizing for them, and trying to make up for them. This is a big part of growing up. That's because every time you take responsibility for your mistakes, you grow up a little:

- You learn not to make the same mistake again, which makes you wiser and safer (and happier).

- You think about why you made the mistake in the first place, which helps you learn more about yourself.

- You set a good example for other kids and earn their respect and friendship.

- You gain more trust and respect for yourself.

Dealing with Serious Mistakes and ----- Repeated Bad Choices -----

If you make a *really* poor choice and do something like steal, take drugs, or start a fight, you can do serious harm to yourself or others. You can end up in trouble with your family, school, and the law. You can still choose to take responsibility for these choices, and, more important, you can choose to stop making them. One of the worst mistakes of all is to keep making poor choices over and over again.

If you get into the habit of making bad choices like these, you can make it harder for others to respect you, or for you to respect yourself. If you've made a serious mistake or think you may be getting into a habit of making wrong choices, talk to an adult you trust. Ask the person to help you. If you don't know how to bring it up, you could say something like, "Dad, can I talk to you? There's something on my mind. I've been hanging out with these kids who steal. I don't feel good about it and I want to change, but I don't know how." Remember, you *can* change!

Part of taking responsibility for bad choices and mistakes is dealing with blame. If you do something wrong, you're likely to hear about it from somebody (you probably don't need me to tell you that). Some people will correct you with kindness when you do something wrong, and others might yell at you in a mean, grouchy voice. It all depends on how the person is feeling and how big the mistake was.

But it doesn't really matter how someone tells you. The important thing is how you react. The tools in this chapter are meant to help you learn to react to blame in a responsible way.

The Mea Culpa

Use the Mea Culpa when you want to make up for something you did.

The Mea Culpa (say it like this: *may-uh cuhl-puh*) is a way of answering people when they blame you for something you did. Mea Culpa means "my fault" in Latin. It means taking responsibility for a mistake you've made, apologizing, and making up for it.

To do the Mea Culpa, you simply tell the truth about what you've done and apologize. You could say something like, "You're right, I did do that, and I'm sorry," or, "You're right, that was a mistake." When you use the Mea Culpa, you are choosing not to argue, get defensive, or make excuses. You are choosing to agree with the person who blamed you and apologize for what you've done.

WAYS TO SAY IT: THE MEA CULPA

Playground duty teacher: *You just broke that window.*
You: *Yeah, I did, and I'm really sorry. Who should I talk to about getting it fixed?*

Your grandmother: *You didn't wash the dishes last night like you were supposed to.*
You: *I know, I'm sorry. I'll wash them the next two nights to make up for it.*

You are also choosing to make up for things. If you have done wrong to someone or something (or yourself), make it better. Take personal responsibility for it. If you cheated on a test, ask the teacher how you can make up for it. If you stole something, return it. Making up for mistakes and not repeating them is the best way to show you're truly sorry.

Imagine you said something really mean to a girl who is a close friend of yours. It may not be enough to say you're sorry. Your friend may still be hurt by what you said, even if you are sorry. To make things right you'll need to show your friend that you care about her. You might say, "I was in a bad mood and took it out on you. I didn't mean what I said at all. I'm lucky to have you as a friend." You might also give her a make-up note or gift to remind her of how much she means to you.

----Steps to the Mea Culpa----

1. Choose to accept responsibility for your actions.

2. Apologize for what you did.

3. Try to make things right again.

MORE WAYS TO SAY IT: THE MEA CULPA

Your principal: *I saw you teasing a student on the playground today.*
You: *You're right, I'm sorry.*
Your principal: *How would you feel if a kid teased you?*
You: *Not good. I'm going to apologize and say something nice to him. And I won't do it again.*

Your teacher: *You flunked your science test today. You need to start studying.*
You: *You're right, I need to do better.*
Your teacher: *You need to work harder.*
You: *I really want to improve. Can you help me? What can I do to study and remember things better?*

The No Way

Use the No Way when you want to tell others you don't deserve blame.

Like the crow, you will sometimes get blamed for things that are not your fault. Sometimes it's a mistake. Somebody thinks you did something—like lying or skipping school—but you didn't. Other times, people may blame you in order to get out of their own responsibility for a mistake or accident. When you know you're not to blame, the No Way can help you say so.

It's just as important to clear yourself of blame you don't deserve as it is to accept blame when you do. If false blame isn't cleared up, you may get into trouble unfairly. You may earn a bad reputation that you don't deserve. This can affect the way people treat you and whether they trust you.

When people incorrectly blame you, use the No Way to stick up for yourself by setting the record straight. Remain calm and don't get defensive. You don't have to actually say, "No way." Instead, you use "no" words like *not* and *didn't*. Clearly and directly, say, "You're wrong, I didn't do that," or, "That's not true."

It might be hard to stay calm if people don't believe you. You may feel more like yelling and stamping your foot. But try not to let your frustration show. Keep control of your emotions and repeat that you are not to blame.

WAYS TO SAY IT: THE NO WAY

Teacher: *Joshua says you stole his apple.*
You: *I didn't steal anything. I wouldn't do that.*
Teacher: *I saw you eating an apple. Are you sure it wasn't Joshua's?*
You: *I'm sure. I brought my own. I don't steal.*

Principal: *Somebody has reported that you picked on some kids at school today.*
You: *It's not true. I didn't pick on anyone.*
Principal: *You'll get in serious trouble if this happened.*
You: *I know that. That's why I don't pick on kids.*

Kid at school: *You're always dropping trash around my locker. You need to knock it off.*
You: *You're wrong. I've never done that.*

Kid: *You're such a messy person. It has to be your stuff.*
You: *It's not.*
Kid: *I don't believe you.*
You: *You don't have to, but I'm telling the truth.*

Don't use this tool unless what you're saying is totally true. If you were to blame for some of the mistake, admit it, but point out the part that's incorrect. If you are completely to blame, you're much better off admitting to it and making up for it rather than lying about it. By being honest you'll be true to yourself and people will learn to trust your word.

MORE WAYS TO SAY IT: THE NO WAY

When you deserve some blame

Your uncle: *I saw that you had a pack of cigarettes in your backpack. We need to talk about this.*
You: *They're not mine. I don't smoke.*
Uncle: *The cigarettes were right there in your backpack.*
You: *I let my friend from school stick them in there so he wouldn't get in trouble.*

Uncle: *That's not very smart. Now you get in trouble.*
You: *You're right, it wasn't too smart. I shouldn't have let him put it in there.*

Teacher: *It looks like you copied your entire report out of the encyclopedia. I'm going to have to give you an F.*
You: *I didn't copy it all. Only the end.*
Teacher: *Even a small part is too much. It's supposed to be your own writing.*
You: *I know, it was wrong to copy. Can I write a new report to make up for it?*

One of the most important things to remember when it comes to the tools of the crow is to tell the truth. It's natural to feel afraid of getting in trouble when you make bad choices or mistakes. But if you lie when you're being blamed, you make it hard for people to believe you in the future. They may think you're lying even when you're not.

You also lose *integrity.* Integrity is being true to yourself and being a good and honest person. It's better to be honest about a mistake and get in trouble than to make the mistake even worse by lying and losing the trust of others—and your integrity.

TaLking Back to Negative Thoughts

THE TOOLS OF THE OWL

Like other birds of prey, owls are calm and focused while waiting to catch their food. But unlike most birds, owls do their hunting at night. That's because they can see and fly really well in the dark (which is bad news if you're a mouse). Sometimes you will have unhappy feelings that make you feel a little dark inside. When you feel dark, it can be hard to stay calm and focused. The tools of the owl can help you see clearly in the dark and not make things worse with what you tell yourself.

So far this book has explained a lot of tools to help you communicate with others. Because people are social, communicating well is very important. It's the best way to improve your chances of getting along with people at school and anywhere else.

But there's something else that's very important: getting along with yourself. That means being comfortable with yourself and understanding your thoughts and feelings.

You have feelings swirling around inside you all the time. For example, you may feel impatient when you're waiting in a long line in the cafeteria. You may feel refreshed when you drink a cold soda on a hot day. You may feel frustrated when you have to learn how to multiply fractions.

Without feelings, you'd be like a robot. You wouldn't know what fun was like. You wouldn't know love, excitement, or kindness. You couldn't enjoy being with your friends or family. You couldn't enjoy playing, dancing, reading, singing, eating, or hanging out. Feelings are like sugar and salt. They give life flavor.

Of course, without feelings you'd also never experience fear, worry, anger, guilt, frustration, sadness, or other unhappy feelings. You might imagine that life would be nice without these types of feelings. But even they are important. Fear can get you to run in times of danger. Worry can push you to take care of something or get ready for the future. Anger can get you to stop others from doing harm. Guilt can help you keep yourself from doing harm. Frustration can lead you to ask for help. And sadness helps you heal when you have to go through really hard times (like losing a loved one).

Unhappy feelings can also help you grow and change as a person. If you don't feel good about something you've done or something that happened to you, you may decide to learn and improve yourself. Unhappy feelings can help you appreciate good times more. And, because everyone goes through hard times and has unhappy feelings, they help you feel connected to other people. When someone else is suffering, you can understand how that person feels. This helps you build strong relationships.

FEELINGS AND THOUGHTS

Every time you cope with unhappy feelings, you are learning and growing. One of the best ways you cope is by using your thoughts. That's because thoughts and feelings are connected. They affect each other.

Consider this example: Let's say you're angry because you think your friend gossiped about you. Your *thought* is that your friend gossiped about you. This thought results in your *feeling* angry. The feeling comes from the thought. Then let's say you find out that she didn't gossip. Your feeling of anger changes, right? That's because getting the facts changed your thought: you know she didn't gossip.

Of course, it's easy to change your thoughts and feelings if you find out you were wrong. So let's look at another example. Let's say you feel lousy because you didn't make the soccer team. What are your thoughts and feelings?

Your **thoughts** are about not making the team.
Your **feelings** are of disappointment.

Only this time you have the facts, and they won't change. You didn't make the team, and that's that.

So, how can you change your feelings? Well, you can still change your thoughts. Instead of thinking about how terrible it is not to make the team, think about more positive things. For example, think about:

- where else you can play soccer (like the playground or your local Boys & Girls Club)

- how some of the best athletes in the world didn't make all of the teams they tried out for

- that you can try out for cross country, instead

    OR

- how, in your humble opinion, they missed out on your very worthy talents and energy!

Your thoughts are very powerful. They can make you feel better or worse. They can make you feel stronger or weaker. Sometimes your thoughts can exaggerate how bad things really are and make you feel worse than you really should. Not making a team is disappointing—especially if it was important to you—and it's normal to feel bad about it. But don't be harder on yourself than you really deserve. Take a look at how Jana reacted when she had a bad day.

When **JANA** got home from school she ran straight to her room, tossed her book bag on the floor, and flopped onto the bed. She stayed there even when her dad called her for dinner. He came up and asked her what was going on.

"I'm *so* embarrassed," Jana said. "I fell in the lunchroom and spilled my tray. There were a hundred people laughing at me. I'm so clumsy and stupid."

"Everybody has accidents sometimes, Jana. It doesn't mean you're clumsy *or* stupid."

"No one has ever had an accident like this, Dad. This was the worst. I can't go back there."

WHEN TO USE THE TOOLS OF THE OWL

Some unhappy feelings can clog up your life, making it harder to get things done or making you feel worse than you really should. When that happens, try to change your feelings by changing your thoughts. Jana probably wouldn't have felt so bad if she had told herself what her dad told her: that it was just an accident. Everyone makes mistakes. It's not always easy to change your thoughts, and there's no magic formula that will make you feel better every time. But if you try to do it, you might surprise yourself. The tools of the owl can help you.

TooL #18

The But Twist

Use the But Twist when you want to overcome thoughts
that keep you from getting things done.

Feelings of helplessness, fear, embarrassment, and worry make it hard to get things done. And if you have thoughts such as "I can't," it's hard to get over those feelings.

For example, if you think your homework is too difficult, and you think, "I can't do it," you'll probably feel afraid to get started or angry that you have to. Those feelings can keep you from doing it. Or if you feel worried about giving a speech in front of your class, a thought that says, "I can't do it," isn't going to help. And you know you have to do these things. If you don't do your homework or give your speech, you'll fail or get a low grade.

The But Twist is a tool that you can use to talk back to "I can't" thoughts—or "I won't" thoughts, "I don't want to" thoughts, or any other thoughts that hold you back. The But Twist means taking the negative thought and *twisting* it around to make it positive with a "but. . . ." For example, say you have a really hard math assignment, and you think, "I don't want to do it." You can use the But Twist to get over that thought. One might be: "I don't want to do it, **but** I can just get started and see how it goes." Or, "**but** I can do all the questions I understand and get help from my brother on the others," or, "**but** the sooner I get it the done, the sooner I can do something else." Any one of those But Twists might get you going.

Practice Time

Here are some common But Twists that can help you talk back to thoughts that keep you from doing things. Practice saying them to yourself in your mind. To really get motivated, say them out loud.

". . . but it'll be nice to have finished."

". . . but it's not really that hard."

". . . but I can get help if I need to."

". . . but I don't have to do it perfectly."

". . . but it won't kill me."

". . . but I can handle it."

". . . but I'll get through it."

". . . but tomorrow I'll feel better." ■

The point of the But Twist is to use a few quick words to get you *doing* whatever needs to be done. If you wait until you *feel* like doing something, you may never do it.

WAYS TO SAY IT: THE BUT TWIST

You have to do research for a report on part of the nervous system. You think:

I don't feel like doing homework . . .

> *but it will be great to have finished.*
>
> *but I actually kind of like science.*
>
> *but it won't take very long.*

Your teacher asks you to clean the board during recess and you feel frustrated. You think:

I'd rather be outside playing . . .

> *but I can play next recess.*
>
> *but it would really help my teacher.*
>
> *but if I do it this time I won't have to do it again for a while.*

A neighbor could use some help shoveling snow off the sidewalk. You think:

It's too cold . . .

> *but it would be a really kind thing to do.*
>
> *but I'll stay warm when I'm shoveling.*
>
> *but it won't take that long.*

You need to go to the dentist. You think:

This freaks me out, I just can't do it . . .

> *but if I don't go, I could have really bad problems with my teeth.*
>
> *but then I won't have to go again for a long time.*
>
> *but it'll be over quickly.*

To get over the feelings that keep you from getting things done, you have to focus on positive thoughts. Twist those "I can't" thoughts around! The more often you do it, the better you'll become.

TooL #19

The Thought Chop

*Use the Thought Chop when you want to talk back
to Things-Are-Terrible thoughts.*

Some unhappy feelings are made worse by what I call Things-Are-Terrible thoughts. Things-Are-Terrible thoughts are thoughts that make you feel more sadness, anger, fear, or other unhappy feelings than you really should. You've probably had these thoughts before . . . thoughts like, "Everybody hates me," "I'm dumb," "I hate life," or, "It's all my fault."

The world stinks.

When you have thoughts like those, you're being too hard on yourself. You can use the Thought Chop to talk back to Things-Are-Terrible thoughts. Thought Chops are words of truth that chop the Things-Are-Terrible thoughts down. Bad things will happen to you at times, but so will good things. The point of the Thought Chop is to remind yourself not to make things worse with what you tell yourself.

Everyone goes through hard times. It's part of life. Some hard times are *really* hard, like if your grandfather dies or you get injured in a car accident. When these hard times happen to you, you have to take time to get over them. But other hard times are not so terrible. Still, they can cause strong, unhappy feelings and make it harder to think clearly. That's when Thinking Mistakes can happen. Thinking Mistakes make hard times seem worse than they are.

5 COMMON THINKING MISTAKES

Here are five types of common Thinking Mistakes that can cause you to feel worse than you need to, along with some examples.

1. Exaggerating

Exaggerating is thinking that something is a lot worse or much more important than it really is.

- We lost the debate, so we have the worst school in the world.

- My friend doesn't like me, so I'll never have a close friend again.

- I always have to do chores, so my foster dad is cruel.

2. Seeing just the bad

Almost nothing that happens to you is all bad. When you see just the bad, you are ignoring things that can help you feel better.

- I have to study at school, so school's no fun.

- We lost the game last night, so we're a terrible team.

- It rained this week, so it was a crummy week.

3. Labeling
Labeling is when you think that because one thing is a certain way, all similar things are that way.

- I have trouble with English, so I'm not a good student.

- I said some dumb things today, so everything I say is dumb.

- The kid from that country is mean, so everyone from his country is mean.

4. Guessing things are bad
This is guessing that something will be bad without really knowing.

- School's going to be boring today.

- I did bad on my last math test, so I'm going to flunk the test today.

- Everyone's going to make fun of the shoes my mom made me wear.

5. Blaming yourself incorrectly

When you blame yourself incorrectly, you take complete personal blame for things, in an extreme way, when you don't deserve it.

- I misspelled *prescient,* so it's my fault our class didn't win the spelling bee.

- I missed the spike, so it's all my fault that we lost the volleyball game.

- The party was at my apartment, so it's my fault some people didn't have fun.

Thinking Mistakes apply not only to how you think about yourself, but how you think about others. Sometimes you may think much worse of people than you should because you exaggerate, label, or see just the bad.

 # Practice Time

Look at the examples for each of the five kinds of Thinking Mistakes on pages 90–92. Now, here are some Thought Chops for dealing with the Thinking Mistakes. See if you can match each Thought Chop to at least one of the examples.

Everyone makes mistakes.

I'll just keep trying.

I studied more this time, so I'll do better.

I can't make somebody have fun. Those kids have to decide for themselves to have fun.

Only I can decide if I'm happy or not.

Our school has lots of good things about it.

I'm a good friend, so I'm sure he'll like me again.

There are mean people from my country, too. That doesn't mean everyone from my country is mean.

Doing dishes isn't so bad.

Nobody can judge me by one thing I did.

The label on my shoes isn't very important, actually.

Nobody's perfect.

I'll get over this.

That was a hard word to spell.

Our team had lots of chances to win. I just missed one chance.

It's not that big of a deal.

We probably just need to practice harder.

It's a team effort, and I'm only one member of the team.

I said some pretty funny and smart things, too.

I'll do better next time. ■

WAYS TO SAY IT: THE THOUGHT CHOP

If you are feeling worse than you need to because of Things-Are-Terrible thoughts, you can use Thought Chops to chop down those unhappy feelings. Here are some examples of hard times, along with the unhappy feelings they might create, and a few Thought Chops to get over them.

Hard time: You get a low grade in English on your report card, and the thought comes, "I'm just dumb. I'm no good with school."

Feeling: You feel disappointed.

Thought Chops: *English isn't my best class, but I do okay in others.*

I can do better than that. I'll try harder next semester.

Just because I got a low grade this time doesn't mean I'm dumb.

Hard time: Some kids in the hall at school point at you and laugh. One of them calls you fat, and a thought comes, "I'm fat, and everyone knows it."

Feeling: You feel ashamed.

Thought Chops: *I may be chubby, but I'm a good person.*

Nobody has a perfect body.

Those kids are really mean, and I wouldn't want to be friends with mean, stuck-up kids anyway.

They need to grow up.

Hard time: You're in a play at school and forget your lines, and you think, "This is the worst day of my life. I'm never doing this again. Everyone must think I'm a dork."

Feeling: You feel embarrassed.

Thought Chops: *I'm really exaggerating, I just forgot a few lines.*

Nobody's perfect. Even the best Hollywood actors forget lines.

It took a lot of guts to stand up in front of everyone.

What's the worst that could happen? (This is a great Thought Chop question. See pages 18–19.)

Hard time: You find out that a boy you like doesn't like you, and the thought comes, "I can never be happy if he doesn't like me."

Feeling: You feel unlovable.

Thought Chops: *I'll get over him.*

It's his loss.

I don't need to be liked by somebody to be happy.

Hard time: You find out that your best friend went with somebody else to see a movie without even asking you. You think, "I hate him. I'm not going to be his friend anymore."

Feeling: You feel angry and hurt.

Thought Chops: *Being friends doesn't mean you have to do every single thing together.*

He invites me to almost everything. Just because he didn't invite me this one time doesn't mean he's a terrible person.

Why would I dump a good friend over something like this?

Hard time: You're not invited to a party that other kids are invited to and you think, "Nobody likes me. I'm a loser."

Feeling: You feel lonely and left out.

Thought Chops: *It would have been fun, but it's their loss.*

I've got plenty of friends.

I'll be invited to other parties.

Remember that most things aren't terrible—they're just a normal part of life. And remember that you don't have to be perfect, beautiful, or popular to be a valued human being. You already are.

TooL #20

SoLution Time 2

Use Solution Time 2 when you want to solve a personal problem that causes you unhappy feelings.

Sometimes changing your thoughts isn't enough to change your unhappy feelings. That might be because you have a bigger problem that needs a real solution. Maybe you're getting bad grades, or you're not getting along with someone in your family, or your friends are spreading mean rumors, or you're having trouble keeping up in science class. There are any number of problems that could affect your feelings. If you can't change your unhappy feelings with your thoughts, you will have to change your actions. That means solving problems.

On pages 44–50 you learned about Solution Time as a way to deal with arguing and fighting. Solution Time 2 is a tool for solving personal problems you have in your own, private life. These may be problems achieving goals or improving yourself or improving a bad situation.

--- Steps for Solution Time 2 ---

1. **Choose to take action.** As with Solution Time, the first step in solving a personal problem is to CHOOSE to solve it. Don't let your unhappy feelings stop you from taking control of your situation. Be a leader with yourself.

2. **Figure out the problem and what you want.** Define exactly what your problem is. Do you need to get out of a group of friends you're not comfortable with? Are your grades too low? Or do you just want to find something to do when you're bored? Then ask yourself how you would

like things to be. If the problem is low grades, what grades do you want? Nothing below a C? Straight A's? Or would you like to do just a little better than you're doing now?

3. **Brainstorm solutions.** This means coming up with as many possible ways to solve the problem as you can. Sometimes it helps to take out a pen and list your solutions on a piece of paper. For example, if you want to solve the problem of getting low grades, and you decide you want to get at least a B in your subjects, you could brainstorm ideas like:

> TALK TO EACH TEACHER ABOUT WHAT I CAN DO
>
> DON'T WATCH ANY TV UNTIL HOMEWORK IS DONE
>
> GO TO EXTRA STUDY TIMES AT SCHOOL
>
> GO TO THE LIBRARY TO STUDY
>
> GET HELP FROM DAD
>
> GET HELP FROM A TUTOR.

4. **Pick a solution and do it.** Choose what you think is the best idea from your list, and call that "Plan A" (your main plan for solving the problem). Then get started. A solution is only a thought until you actually start doing it. This may take some determination and a few But Twists . . . but you can do it!

5. **If you need help, get it.** Everybody needs help sometimes, especially with really serious or difficult problems. Don't feel bashful about asking others for help in talking about problems, coming up with solutions, or following through on them.

- -

Once you get started solving problems, you'll probably notice how good it feels. Problem-solving is a wonderful power to have, and it can be rewarding and fun.

TooL #21

The BaLLoon BeLLy

*Use the Balloon Belly when you want
to feel calm and relaxed.*

It can be a lot easier to get over the unhappy feelings that clog up your life if you're calm. Calmness makes it easier for happy feelings to come instead. It's like you're making a space for happy feelings to fill up.

Part of feeling calm is using the Thought Chop to talk back to Thinking Mistakes that upset you. But another way to feel calm is by relaxing your body and mind. There are many ways to do this, including:

- playing a game
- going for a walk
- listening to relaxing music

- watching a movie
- lounging around
- napping
- reading
- talking on the telephone
- playing with a pet.

It's usually a lot easier to relax your body than your mind. You can often lie down or sit back, but your mind may keep on busily working. Sometimes it's hard to let go of anger, frustration, or other strong thoughts and feelings. If you need help calming your mind, try the Balloon Belly. The Balloon Belly is a way of using your breath to help you blow away troubling thoughts and feelings.

Steps for
------- the Balloon Belly -------

1. Find a comfortable position. You can do the Balloon Belly sitting down, standing in a line, or lying on your couch.

2. Take a deep breath in through your nose.

3. Count to five, then let it out through your mouth.

4. Listen to your breath. Pay attention to nothing else.

When you breathe in, your stomach should go out, like a balloon filling with air. When you breathe out, it should go in, like a balloon deflating. Each time you breathe out, imagine all the thoughts and feelings that make it hard to relax are flowing out of your body along with your breath. It might help to close your eyes or put your hands on your stomach.

Your breath is like the waves of the ocean or a big lake. When you pay attention, breathing in sounds a little like waves coming into shore, and breathing out sounds like waves going out to sea. As you're practicing the Balloon Belly, remember to focus all of your attention on your breathing. That helps take your mind off the other thoughts that keep it busy. Every time a thought of worry, fear, or anger comes to you, blow out the thought (and the feeling that comes with it) and return to noticing the warm, cozy feeling and sound of your breath.

In everyday life, it doesn't make sense to spend too much time with thoughts or feelings that make you feel unhappy. The less time the better. Pay attention when you have these kinds of thoughts and feelings. If you don't need them, use the Balloon Belly to let them go, just like you might let go of a balloon high into the sky.

What If You Have Negative Thoughts or Feelings
------ That Won't Go Away? ------

Sometimes negative thoughts or feelings, like sadness or anger, stay with people and don't go away. Do you feel helpless or hopeless? Do you feel sadness that goes on and on? Do you feel like hurting yourself or others? Are you very anxious or nervous all the time? If any of these sound like what you're feeling, get some help right away. Talk to an adult you trust or look in the yellow pages under Crisis Intervention or the back of the white pages under First Call for Help. Or you can call the toll-free National Hopeline Network: 1-800-442-HOPE (4673).

Getting along with yourself can be every bit as hard as getting along with others. When you feel like you are in dark times, use the tools of the owl to help you see clearly—and to find bright times again.

Some Final Thoughts

This book provides you with tools to help you get along with people at school. I know that school can be a stressful part of kids' lives, and my hope is that *Speak Up and Get Along!* can make it a little less so. But getting along isn't just about taking care of yourself when you have social problems. It's about kids working together. You can make a big difference at your school by being kind to others, being respectful, and saying, "Knock it off," to kids who are mean to others. Every student deserves to feel safe, respected, and comfortable in school. In the same way that flocks of birds cooperate with each other and help other members of the flock, you can help other members of your school.

Also, give some thought to who you hang out with. Do you have friends who are respectful of you, your teachers, and others? Do you have friends who are serious about school? Be smart about who you choose to be your friends. Good friends make school easier and more fun because they respect you and you respect them. They appreciate you for who you are. They also take your side when you need them.

Sometimes you'll need help from adults. At school, teachers, principals, counselors, and psychologists are there to help you when you need it. That's their job. There are also adults who care about you at home, in sports or clubs, at after-school programs, and in your faith community. Make sure to talk to an adult if you are having social problems and you don't know how to fix them.

Finally, ask your teacher or an adult at home to read the "Note to Adults" that follows this chapter. Then talk to that adult about problems or questions you have about getting along with others. You can practice the tools with adults and even learn new ones from them. More people care about you than you may realize. We're all pulling for you to be happy, successful, and able to *Speak Up and Get Along!*

Note to Adults

As parents, guardians, and teachers, we are the people from whom our children will learn most of what they know about getting along with others. In the book *Best Friends, Worst Enemies,* Michael Thompson, et al., make an analogy between how we support our children as they learn to swim and how we can support them in their social worlds. When they are quite young, we wade into the water with them. We let them swirl around a bit, holding onto our hands, and we let them tippy-toe along by themselves in the shallow end of the pool. When they get older we give them some formal instruction, and they get more comfortable with the water. We are still in the pool with them, but they do much more on their own. Eventually they swim completely on their own. But even then we continue to watch them from the sides of the pool, and we jump in as a lifeguard if they have trouble.

Teaching kids to socialize is much the same. When they are very young—babies and toddlers—we wade into the "pool" with them. We help them through their early social situations by carrying them along, always being present. Later, we give them some instruction. We teach them to share and be polite, to be fair and think of other people's feelings—basically, to get along with other kids. We are still there with them, and we intervene when needed to make sure they're okay. Eventually we send them to school, and here they swim through the social waters on their own.

But we can still be lifeguards, even then. To take it a step further, we can be coaches. Indeed, this is probably the most important thing we can do to help children get along at school, and in the rest of their social world. We can continue coaching them, teaching them what we know, helping them with their problems, and jumping in to save them if things get dangerous.

PRACTICING WITH CHILDREN

The tools and skills taught in *Speak Up and Get Along!* are best learned by a child through the guidance of an adult. Be sure to read this book before you give it to a child.

There is ample evidence to support the idea that role playing and talking to children about their social experiences can help them become much better at coping with difficult social situations—especially when it comes to dealing with teasing and conflict. They also need encouragement to stick with their efforts. This book provides example dialogs and scenarios—as well as discussions of why people may act and feel the way they do—that can be used as starting points for adults to talk and practice with children.

In addition to practicing the example dialogs with children, practice ad lib situations, too, and trade off roles. For example, you might first play the role of one of the child's peers, pressuring your child or student to do something she or he doesn't want to do. Then, let the child play the role of a peer while you play the child's part. This gives him or her the benefit of seeing how you would handle certain situations, and also helps show what kinds of assertive responses are most effective from the peer's perspective.

Within the classroom, this book can provide the groundwork for discussions on social interaction. Some teachers create posters of each bird as starting points for discussions of each category of social skill development. They solicit the thoughts and experiences of students during classroom time. Then they demonstrate the skills and provide students with time to practice the social skills with each other. These sessions don't have to use up much class time.

TEACHING CHILDREN TO BE ASSERTIVE AND SOLVE PROBLEMS

Assertiveness is being direct, but not aggressive. There is a great deal we can do to help children develop assertive social and problem-solving skills. Here are some of the key areas in which we can positively influence children's development of these skills.

1. Living environment

- Develop a warm relationship with the children for whom you have responsibility. Talk to them, listen to them, support them in their school activities, show interest in the things that matter to them, and do fun things together.

- Encourage open, direct communication in the home by not punishing or being dismissive of children when they ask questions. Be open and direct yourself by telling children exactly what you want and how you feel.

- Allow for assertiveness that's respectful.

- Allow for expression of both good and bad feelings as long as it's done respectfully.

- Rein in physical and verbal aggression.

- Don't overprotect timid children by shielding them from social interaction or intervening with every social difficulty (unless bullying, hitting, or safety are involved).

- Promote healthy social connections and interactions. Parents should encourage children to invite other children to the home to play, and enroll children in social groups and activities.

2. Modeling

- Solve problems in the family or classroom using good communication and problem-solving skills. Provide an example during conflicts by using direct, non-hostile communication and sitting down to have Solution Time (as described on pages 44–50 of this book).

- Correct children by simply expressing what you want rather than belittling them, nagging them, or making them feel guilty. Make it clear it's the behavior you're reacting to, not the child.

- Demonstrate assertive communication skills when dealing with others outside of the family.

3. Discussing

- Take the time to listen to and understand children's social experience. What's happening at school? Who are their friends? How do they enjoy school beyond the classes?

- Help give them perspective, let them know of your own experiences, and help them respond to counterproductive beliefs or thinking habits. Saying things like, "We'll get over it," "Let's figure out how to solve this together," "Everyone makes mistakes," "Don't be too hard on yourself," and, "This is a normal part of life," can be immensely helpful coming from an authority figure.

- Develop solutions to problems together.

4. Coaching and practicing

- Share your own real-life experiences and teach your own verbal tools and strategies. How did you deal with teasing, bullying, and shyness when you were a kid? How did you feel when you had to undergo those experiences?

- Practice everyday situations through role playing using the scripts in this book and real situations your children or students are going through.

- Give them the same encouragement that you'd give for any other difficult endeavor. Just as in teaching a child how to ride a bike, help them work through the "I can't do it, it's not working" phase with further practice and follow-up.

5. "Lifeguarding"

- Pay attention to what's going on with the children for whom you have responsibility. Know where they are, who they're with, and what they're doing. Parents and teachers should communicate regularly.

- Jump in and save them when they are struggling or are in danger. Assertively speak to other parents and children if necessary.

HELPING CHILDREN DEAL WITH BULLYING

Bullying is an issue where kids need particular help. Bullying in schools is pervasive. According to a 2001 study done by the Kaiser Family Foundation, almost three-quarters of preteens said bullying is a regular occurrence at school. The LaMarsh Centre for Research on Violence and Conflict Resolution at York University conducted a study in which 35 percent of children studied reported they were involved in the bullying cycle (either as bullies or victims). (For more information on these studies and statistics, see *The Bully, the Bullied, and the Bystander* by

Barbara Coloroso.) A poll conducted by KidsHealth revealed that 48 percent of kids had been bullied before. Many more are witnesses to bullying.

Victims of bullying frequently experience a drop in grades, acute despair, chronic illness, and isolation. But putting an end to bullying doesn't only help the victim. It also helps the bully. A high percentage of children who bully end up with adult criminal records (Beane 115). Here are some things adults can do to help solve this serious social problem.

What teachers and school administrators can do

1. Take bullying seriously and don't accept it. Part of the problem is attitudinal—lack of resolve and determination in ending it in the school environment. It's critical to be swift in investigations and disciplinary actions relating to bullying.

2. Establish a reasonable but strict code of conduct when it comes to harmful behavior (including sexual and racial harassment). A school bullying policy should be posted in each classroom and discussed in class meetings at the beginning of each new quarter or semester. The policy should clearly define what constitutes bullying, the obligation of all students to report bullying, the investigation process, and disciplinary consequences.

3. Provide good supervision, including a "student watch" program and/or video surveillance if necessary. Poor supervision and lack of decisive response can be the most critical factors in fostering bullying in schools.

4. Train teachers and aides how to recognize bullying and what to do about it.

5. Encourage anonymous reporting by students. Promote this as a responsibility. (Schools that do this are sometimes called "telling schools.")

6. Establish programs that help develop social connections and group support, such as "buddy" programs (pairing students from upper grades with lower grades) and Tribes (a program in the United States and Canada that teaches children to participate in groups and support each other—see Resources, page 116).

7. Make teaching and practicing social and problem-solving skills (including conflict resolution) part of the curriculum.

8. Provide professional counseling and guidance (not just discipline) for kids involved in bullying behavior.

What parents and guardians can do

1. Using the tools in this book and other skills or tools, teach your child to become a less-likely victim of bullying as well as how to stop bullying once it begins.

2. Intervene when necessary (with school personnel, administration or board members, other parents, or counselors) if a bullying situation with your child is not getting resolved at school or in the neighborhood.

3. In extreme cases, move your child into a new school, contact police, or take legal action.

It's hard to see a child you care about struggle with social situations, but most children do at one time or another. Parents, guardians, and teachers are in a better position to help children than anyone else. Model respectful social behavior and show kids that you respect them. Practice the tools in this book with them. Listen when they talk. And keep the lines of communication open between home and school. Help make getting along with others easier, and more fun, for the children you care about.

Resources for Kids

Bullying Is a Pain in the Brain, by Trevor Romain, illustrated by Steve Mark (Minneapolis: Free Spirit Publishing, 2016). If you need more help making yourself bully-proof, here's a funny but useful book with lots of good tips.

The Feelings Book: The Care and Keeping of Your Emotions, by Lynda Madison, illustrated by Norm Bendell (Middleton, WI: Pleasant Company, 2002). This book, part of the American Girl Library, explains emotions and provides suggestions for handling powerful feelings and developing positive self-esteem.

From Boys to Men: All About Adolescence and You, by Michael Gurian (New York: Price Stern Sloan, Inc.: 1999). This book discusses the physical, mental, and emotional changes that boys go through during adolescence, providing practical advice and answering the tough questions.

How Kids Make Friends: Secrets for Making Lots of Friends, No Matter How Shy You Are, by Lonnie Michelle. (Buffalo Grove, IL: Freedom Publishing Company, 1997). This popular book teaches kids social skills and helps you to gain confidence and make and keep friends.

KidsHealth
www.kidshealth.org
Click "Kids site," then "Feelings." You can learn more about getting along, bullying, peer pressure, shyness, and a lot of other topics that are important to kids.

School Conflict, by Tish Davidson (New York: Franklin Watts, 2003). This book looks at violence in schools, including bullying and harrassment. It discusses reasons school violence happens, what people are doing to prevent it, and what kids can do about it.

Shykids.com
www.shykids.com
This Web site provides a lot of helpful advice for building confidence, making friends, talking to grown-ups, and overcoming shyness. Click on "Chit-Chat" for more examples of phrases you can use to start and continue conversations. The site also has a lot of cool links to other sites where you can learn about social activities and groups.

Stick Up for Yourself! Every Kid's Guide to Personal Power and Positive Self-Esteem, by Gershen Kaufman, Ph.D., Lev Raphael, Ph.D., and Pamela Espeland (Minneapolis: Free Spirit Publishing, 1999). Simple words and real-life examples show how you can stick up for yourself with other kids, big sisters and brothers, and grown-ups, too.

Resources for Parents and Teachers

Best Friends, Worst Enemies: Understanding the Social Lives of Children, by Michael Thompson, Lawrence J. Cohen, and Catherine O'Neill-Grace (New York: Ballantine, 2002). This book describes the social lives of children and provides insights into what both parents and teachers can do to help children manage social difficulties.

The Bully, the Bullied, and the Bystander: From Preschool to High School—How Parents and Teachers Can Help Break the Cycle of Violence, by Barbara Coloroso (New York: HarperCollins, 2004). Coloroso breaks down destructive myths about bullying and provides real, practical ways to help adults protect their children. She also provides advice for helping bullies change and for urging bystanders to speak out against the bullying and stand up for their peers.

The New Bully Free Classroom: Proven Prevention and Intervention Strategies for Teachers K–8 (Updated Edition), by Allan L. Beane, Ph.D. (Minneapolis: Free Spirit Publishing, 2011). A comprehensive resource for creating a peaceful, caring classroom that promotes a sense of belonging in all students and stops bullying in its tracks. Beane's prevention and intervention strategies focus on classroom attitudes, thinking, and behavior; on students who are or could become victims of bullies; and on bullies themselves. Positive and practical, the book is reinforced with true stories and by reproducible forms, checklists, and resources.

Bullying at School, by Dan Olweus (Malden, MA: Blackwell Publishing, 1993). Based on the Olweus's own large-scale studies, this book is a milestone in the study of bullying at school and essential reading for all who are involved with young people.

No Kidding About Bullying: 126 Ready-to-Use Activities to Help Kids Manage Anger, Resolve Conflicts, Build Empathy, and Get Along by Naomi Drew (Minneapolis: Free Spirit Publishing, 2017). This flexible resource gives educators and youth leaders a diverse range of activities they can use to help kids in grades 3–6 build empathy, manage anger, work out conflicts, and be assertive.

Emotional Intelligence: Why It Can Matter More Than IQ, by Daniel Goleman (New York: Bantam Books, 1997). Goleman's groundbreaking book explores what he calls "emotional intelligence," a way of being smart that goes beyond IQ. Emotional intelligence includes self-awareness and impulse control, persistence, zeal and self-motivation, empathy, and social deftness. This book provides great insight into our emotions, ways to work with our emotions, and practical ways to nurture emotional intelligence in children.

How to Talk So Kids Will Listen & Listen So Kids Will Talk, by Adele Faber and Elaine Mazlish (New York: HarperResource, 1999). This book provides a step-by-step approach to improving family relationships and parents' ability to talk and problem-solve with children.

KidsHealth
www.kidshealth.org
Click on "Parents site," then choose from many categories, such as "Emotions & Behavior" and "School & Family Life," to access dozens of articles on a wide range of topics that will help you understand—and care for—your child better.

Schools Where Everyone Belongs, by Stan Davis (Champaign, IL: Research Press, 2005). An excellent resource that provides step-by-step strategies for implementing whole-school programs to counter bullying and harassment.

Sticks and Stones: 7 Ways Your Child Can Deal with Teasing, Conflict, and Other Hard Times, by Scott Cooper (New York: Three Rivers Press, 2000). A resource to help parents teach their children how to deal with difficult social situations. The book uses many of the same tools taught in *Speak Up and Get Along!* in a format meant for parents.

Tribes Learning Community:
A New Way of Learning and Being Together
www.tribes.com
Tribes TLC® is a process for creating a positive classroom or school environment. Children work together in long-term groups (tribes) to help each other work on tasks, set goals and solve problems, monitor and assess progress, and celebrate achievements. Go to the Tribes Web site to learn more about this program or sign up for training.

Using Peer Mediation in Classrooms and Schools: Strategies for Teachers, Counselors, and Administrators, by James Gilhooley and Nannette S. Scheuch (Thousand Oaks, CA: Corwin Press, 2000).This guide offers educators, students, and parents a step-by-step process for implementing a peer mediation program in elementary and secondary schools. The book includes role-playing scripts and training posters.

Index

About the Author

Scott Cooper is an anti-bullying advocate and has provided workshops on the topic throughout northern California. He has been a school board president and member of the Sonoma County Advisory Board of Drug Programs. Scott has past experience teaching, coaching basketball, and working as a bilingual aide. He is CFO of a planning and design firm and a member of the National Audubon Society. He is the author of *Sticks and Stones: 7 Ways Your Child Can Deal with Teasing, Conflict, and Other Hard Times* (Three Rivers Press, 2000).

Other Great Books from Free Spirit

Stick Up for Yourself!

Every Kid's Guide to Personal Power and Positive Self-Esteem
Revised and Updated

by Gershen Kaufman, Ph.D., Lev Raphael, Ph.D., and Pamela Espeland

Realistic, encouraging, how-to advice for kids on being assertive, building relationships, becoming responsible, growing a "feelings vocabulary," making good choices, solving problems, setting goals, and more. For ages 8–12.
128 pp.; PB; illust.; 6" x 9"

Stand Up to Bullying!

(Upstanders to the Rescue!)

by Phyllis Kaufman Goodstein and Elizabeth Verdick

Who has the most power to stop and prevent bullying? Teachers? Parents? The Principal of the Universe? No, no, and no way! When it comes to changing bullying behavior, nobody has more power than upstanders—all the people who see bullying or know it's happening . . . and decide to do something about it. With full-color cartoons and humorous, kid-friendly text, *Stand Up to Bullying!* teaches kids how to safely take a stand against bullying, support kids who are targeted, and spread the word that bullying is not cool—it's cruel. For ages 8–13.
128 pp.; PB; color illust.; 5⅛" x 7"

Bullying Is a Pain in the Brain

(Revised & Updated Edition)

by Trevor Romain, illustrated by Steve Mark

This updated classic reassures kids that bullying is not their fault and describes realistic ways to become "Bully-Proof." With humor and practical suggestions, it shows how bystanders can stand up for others, how to get help in dangerous situations, and how kids who bully can start to get along with others and feel good about themselves. For ages 8–13. *112 pp.; PB; color illust.; 5⅛" x 7"*

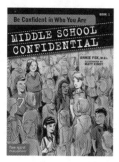

Be Confident in Who You Are

Middle School Confidential™ Series, Book 1
by Annie Fox, M.Ed., illustrated by Matt Kindt

The first book in the Middle School Confidential series follows Jack, Jen, Chris, Abby, Mateo, and Michelle as they work to meet new challenges and survive the social scene—without losing sight of who they are. Readers get information on common challenges and practical advice for being healthy, feeling good about who they are, and staying in control of feelings and actions—even when the pressure is on. Features graphic-novel-style illustrations, quotes, quizzes, tips, tools, and resources. For ages 11–14. *96 pp.; PB; color illust.; 6" x 8"*

The Survival Guide for Making and Being Friends
by James J. Crist, Ph.D.

Whether kids find socializing as natural as smiling or as hard as learning a foreign language, this book can help them improve their social skills so they can better enjoy the benefits of friendship. Practical advice covers everything from breaking the ice to developing friendships to overcoming problems. True-to-life vignettes, "what would you do?" scenarios, voluminous examples, quizzes to test learning, "Try This" assignments for practicing techniques, and advice from real kids make this an accessible life-skills handbook. For ages 8–13. *128 pp.; PB; 2-color; illust.; 6" x 9"*

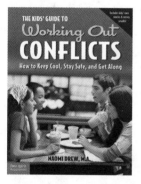

The Kids' Guide to Working Out Conflicts

How to Keep Cool, Stay Safe, and Get Along
by Naomi Drew, M.A.

Proven ways to avoid conflict and defuse tough situations, written by an expert on conflict resolution and peacemaking. Kids learn how to stand up for themselves without getting physical, how to talk out problems, how to de-stress and calm down, how to deal with teasing and bullying, how to stay safe, and more—essential life skills for all young people. For ages 10–15. *160 pp.; PB; 2-color; illust.; 7" x 9"*

Interested in purchasing multiple quantities and receiving volume discounts?
Contact edsales@freespirit.com or call 1.800.735.7323 and ask for Education Sales.

Many Free Spirit authors are available for speaking engagements, workshops, and keynotes.
Contact speakers@freespirit.com or call 1.800.735.7323.

For pricing information, to place an order, or to request a free catalog, contact:

Free Spirit Publishing Inc.
6325 Sandburg Road • Suite 100 • Minneapolis, MN 55427-3674
toll-free 800.735.7323 • local 612.338.2068
fax 612.337.5050 • help4kids@freespirit.com • www.freespirit.com